"Humorous Adventures with Baaaaahbra!!!"

Barbara Gross

COPYRIGHT 2018

ALL RIGHTS RESERVED

NO PART OF THIS PUBLICATION MAY BE REPRODUCED, STORED IN A RETRIEVAL SYSTEM, OR TRANSMITTED IN ANY FORM OR BY ANY MEANS, ELECTRONIC, MECHANICAL, PHOTOCOPY, RECORDING, OR ANY OTHER, WITHOUT THE PRIOR WRITTEN PERMISSION OF THE AUTHOR.

TABLE OF CONTENTS

Acknowledgements 7
Foreword 9
Introduction... 11
Chapter 1: Communication..…..13
Chapter 2: Growing Up Gross: The Early Years 23
Chapter 3: Growing Up Gross: The Pre-Teenage Years ..29
Chapter 4: Growing Up Gross: From High School to College 33
Chapter 5: Growing up Gross—Boyfriend Dating Adventures 43
Chapter 6: The Ultimate Sportswoman 50
Chapter 7: First Jobs 59
Chapter 8: Things Happen For A Reason.......................... 67
Chapter 9: Las Vegas... 80
Chapter 10: Having It My Way... 84
Chapter 11: Traveling Adventures in the US 89
Chapter 12: My Moscow Adventures 98
Chapter 13: Birthday Moments... 106
Chapter 14: My "Granny" 112
Reviews... 118
About the Author... 123

Acknowledgements

I would like to thank all of my relatives and friends (who were mentioned) in contributing to the stories, as without them, there would not be any stories.

A Very Special Thanks To:

My Mother, who has always guided me lovingly with unconditional love and is my best friend. She has always been available to be supportive and cheer me on for that next opportunity!!!

My Father, who always showed me unconditional love, was my protector and always made me feel secure and protected, "Daddy's Girl"!!!

My Brother, Steven, who taught me the merits of eating organic and has been very supportive with his feedback and ideas!!!

And last but not least, My Brother, Danny, who has influenced a lot of these stories, contributed to what my sense of humor is today, showing unconditional love and ready to be by my side at a moment's notice who has been my rock!!!

They deserve a lot of credit as they had to put up with me for the better part of 60 years. I guess someone had to do it!!! :>)

Foreword

I have been a fan of Baaaaahbra since I first met her. She has always uplifted my spirits, brought a smile to my heart and has a contagious joyful energy that she carries everywhere she goes. Every once in a while, we get to meet someone that brings laughter, warmth and joy with her...every conversation, interaction, and share.

I was so excited when she shared about this powerful book that she wanted to share with the world and our organization is truly honored to support her in publishing it. Personally, I am truly honored to know Baaaaahbra and I know that this book will uplift you, bring a smile to your heart and face, and joy to your spirit. As a heart centered comedian, authentic best-selling author, uplifting TV Show Host, and joy-filled speaker she is making a powerful impact for good in the world.

As an Empowerment Leader, Publisher, Author, Network Owner, and Speaker, I have discovered our perspective matters. It effects how we see things, events, ourselves and others. When we can tap into our joy, find humor, laugh, and treat life as a rich and powerful adventure it not only empowers and uplifts us but all of those around us. I love how Baaaaahbra is able to lift up and empower others through how she looks at life…and shares about it.

I know you will be encouraged, as you enjoy her adventures and unique perspective on life. We hope her book will inspire you to bring another perspective to your own adventures in life. Are you treating your life story as things that are happening to you? Or are you finding the silver lining, humor in the unexpected, and discovering the joy you can bring and choose to see each step along the way. We can't always choose what happens to us but we can choose our response.

I know you will enjoy Baaaaahbra's heart-warming adventures, relate to part of the journey, and be inspired to bring a positive perspective to your life's path. Enjoy, smile, laugh deeply (and loudly ☺) as you enjoy **"Humorous Adventures with Baaaaahbra!!!"** by my good friend, Barbara Gross.

Rebecca Hall Gruyter, Empowerment Leader

CEO of RHG Media Productions, RHG TV Network, and Your Purpose Driven Practice.

www.YourPurposeDrivenPractice.com

www.RHGTVNetwork.com

Rebecca@YourPurposeDrivenPractice.com

(925) 787-1572

Introduction

I am honored that Rebecca Hall Gruyter from RHG Media Productions wanted to publish my book. She has opened so many doors for me and I thank her very much for giving me an opportunity to express myself in multiple mediums.

This book was written from the pages of my life as I was growing up Barbara Gross.

I am hoping I can bring levity to daily challenges you might experience in everyday life to acknowledge that you have a choice on how you react to any situation. I believe I have fine-tuned my laughter muscle so that I can embrace the unexpected. What do you choose???

In sharing some of my stories with you about miscommunication and resolving misunderstandings with humor, I hope to brighten your day and give you an expanded way of looking at the world. I have discovered that being able to laugh at oneself is great fun and a powerful way to step forward in life!!!

Even though certain incidents are happening to me, I believe that everyone can relate to these stories. In reading, you may recognize yourself in the same situations or picture yourself in one of these situations. What did/would you do??? Did you choose to embrace the situation and reflect??? Everyone makes mistakes and I believe you can learn from them and then hopefully laugh about them, as well. When people meet me, they always ask, "Why do all of these funny things happen to you???" I reply, "if you listen carefully, some things weren't so funny at the time but in hindsight, they are hysterical!!!'

I am basically expressing my love of life using humor as my vehicle. I truly know what unconditional love is as it was given to me on Day One and I knew I was always loved. Most of the passages in this book explain how when things may go wrong, try to make the best of the situation and be an optimist. I do believe in miracles and I hope they find me, as well as, each of you reading this book. I know that at times life can get bleak but I don't think it makes matters any better if you make yourself upset. Try looking at the situation in a positive way as I believe you can choose your perspective and response. You get to choose what you echo out into the world. I invite you to share out positive vibrations and they will come back to you. Only good things can come from having a positive attitude as you are working through a difficult situation.

I have learned that being my authentic self is what I want to be and show others why that is valuable. May you enjoy these adventures. I hope they brighten your day, expand your heart, and bring joy on your journey through life.

Chapter 1
Communication

Did you ever say something and others heard something else???

Let me share with you some of my experiences with communication.

As the saying goes, by Ralph Waldo Emerson, "Life Is A Journey, Not A Destination." I believe you have a choice to either laugh or cry and I choose to laugh.

People often ask me "Why do all of these funny things keep happening to you???" I reply, "If you listen carefully, they really were not that funny at the time, but in hindsight, they are hysterical!!!" I hope you enjoy some of these moments and life lessons I learned along the way.

My Boston Accent:

The minute I open my mouth, people ask me where I am from and I reply that I am from Boston and my accent will have to be surgically removed!!! The closer you live to Boston, the stronger the accent and I grew up five minutes north of Boston.

Words that I say that will sound different are any words that have the letter "A" before the letter "R" because I will say these words without pronouncing the "AR" and it will sound more like "AH", for example, CAR=CAH, PARK=PAHK, HARVARD=HAHVAHD YARD= YAHD.

No R's:

I was student teaching third and fourth graders in Western Massachusetts where they do not have an accent and the spelling word was "CAR", I pronounced it as "CAH" so the students yelled out, "What is that word???" (As if they didn't know). I said, "It is another word for automobile and if you don't get it right, it's not my problem."

I also say some words the same, for example, "Car Keys" and "Khakis" (as in Khaki Pants). The way I will say it would be, "Cah Keys" and "Cahkeys".

I learned a long time ago that you learn most of your vocabulary by the age of nine. So, I try to find creative ways to help bridge the gap and help people understand what I'm trying to share with them. Here is an interesting example: When I think of my friend's father "Carl" while growing up in Boston, I would pronounce his name as "Cahl". Once I moved to California, I was introduced to a hamburger place called, "Carl's Jr". To this day, when I think of my friend's father, I say, "Cahl" and when I think of the hamburger place, I say, "Carl". So, it is not that I cannot say "R's" but it is how I grew up saying the word.

The other day, I decided that I wanted to order a pizza via telephone and they asked, "What is your name???" I replied, "Baaaaahbra." They tried to repeat me and asked, "Bob???" I replied again, "Baaaaahbra." They said, "What???" I then said, "Forget it, Cindy, I'll be there!!!" Sometimes you've just got to focus more on the result than always being on the same page. ☺

A "J" is supposed to sound like an "H"???

Since I was the youngest of my family, once I was living away at college my parents thought they could retire to a warmer climate. If you are from New England and are ready to retire, you usually go to Florida. So, that is what my parents did. However, it was just too humid for my father. So, they decided to move to California. They told me that they actually found a nice place to live in La Jolla. Now, they pronounced it just as it is spelled instead of how you are supposed to pronounce it, LaHoya. What did we know about pronouncing "J's" like "H's", we are from Boston??? So, when I graduated college, I wanted to check out La Jolla and sure enough, I liked it. When I went to a Mexican restaurant, I asked the waiter, "What are these things Jalapenos???" He replied, "They are Halapenos". Okay, once again, how would I know about the "J" sounding like an "H"???"

We all have the opportunity to learn the unwritten rules of communication as we go. Be open to connection, true communication, and remember to laugh and enjoy the journey.

Please Repeat:

One important lesson I learned in communication is to remember to ask people to repeat what they actually heard. Misunderstandings can create a funny and unexpected connections and conversations.

For example, one time a guy asked me if I played tennis. I replied, "Well, I'm not that good but I have great effort." Suddenly, he had a very funny look on his face. Well, I know what I said and it did not deserve a face contortion. I asked him, "What do you think I just said to you???" He replied, "Well, I'm not that good but I have a great outfit." I love to ask people to repeat things if I see they did not understand me as it is so funny!!!

Plus, I discovered it helps with communication to make sure what you are saying is truly being heard. For example, one time my boyfriend was working in his yard and I was "supervising" as I usually do. The job of supervisor, by my definition, is to make sure that while he is toiling in the yard on those hot summer days that I am nearby in my supervisor's chair in the shade sipping my iced tea available to give him a cold beverage when needed. This one day I was supervising, I decided that I needed to keep my feet up so I retrieved another chair to lay my feet on. When my boyfriend took a break to sit by me, he noticed that I was scratching my legs and hives seemed to be forming. He asked me, "What are those red bumps on your legs???" I said, "I think I am allergic to the Cheer." He said, "How can you be allergic to the chair???" I said, "Not the chair, the Cheer, you know the laundry detergent." Again, repeating back helps us determine what has been heard versus what we are trying to say.

Another time, my boyfriend and I starting to really enjoy learning and watching "Texas Hold'em". "Texas Hold'em" is a poker game that we would watch on TV and also play with our friends. We decided that we wanted to buy a book of poker strategies so I went up to the clerk in the bookstore to see what books they might have in stock and where they would be located in the store. The clerk was taking a very long time reviewing the information on his computer screen. I asked, "Is there a problem, are you not finding any titles???" He said, "No, I have found some titles but they are all out of print." I could not understand this as "Texas Hold'em" was very popular at the time and I would see current advertisements to buy these books. So, I asked again, "Are you sure there are no books currently available for poker??? May I look at the screen you are looking at???" He turned his monitor around and what do you know...He was looking for books on polka dancing not poker. My accent got me again. I have discovered it's important to stop, pause and check in to make sure we are understanding each other. If I see confused looks or something doesn't make sense in their response to me.... it's well worth taking the extra step to stop and check in before pushing forward and creating even more confusion and misunderstandings.

After doing a number of trade shows in Las Vegas. The man who built the booths for our company decided to take the event manager and me to Caesars Palace and buy us the best and most expensive red wine they had to offer in appreciation of giving his company our business. My friend and I got there a little early and decided to start out with a glass of their house red wine. Our host then shows up and again offers to buy us the best and most expensive red wine Caesars Palace had to offer. I said to him, "I appreciate the offer and it's a wonderful gesture but I only know the difference between rot gut and medium wine. When you get to the real expensive stuff, what do I know???" He said, "What a wino???" I said, "Yes, whata I know???" He said, "What a wino???" I said, "Yes, whata I know???" Until it finally donned on me what we were both saying. I later told my company about it and since they have such a great sense of humor, they gave me a plaque as an award with it spelled both ways: "What a wino" and "Whata I know." It's important when you get into a circular response conversation like this to stop and see if perhaps you are actually not saying the same thing after all.

Regional Differences:

In Boston, if you ask for a regular coffee, you get a coffee with cream and sugar. When I was in western Massachusetts, I ordered a regular coffee and received a black coffee. I told them that this was not a regular coffee and they said it was regular and not decaf. It just goes to show, not only accents, but that we also use many different regional terms.

In some regions, a long sandwich might be called a" submarine sandwich" or a "grinder" or a "hoagie" and a "sofa" could be called a "couch" in other regions. You want to make sure you understand where you are as well as what you are trying to say, order, and communicate.

I was once teaching a business class for young adults in California and happened to yell out, "Does anyone have an elastic???" There were looks of surprise and somewhat horror that I would yell something like that out in a classroom. I realized that once again my accent or different regional terminology must have come into play again but I could not imagine what the faux pas was this time. A little later, one of my students asked me why I would yell out if anyone in class had a condom. I guess I should have said, rubber band instead of elastic, who knew???

Another time I worked for a company in the UK. Even though, we are both speaking English, some words mean different things, for example, a "lift" in the UK is an "elevator". In the USA, a "lift" could be "getting a ride". The "queue" is where you stand in line in the UK. In the USA, a "cue" is something you use to play the game of pool as in "pool cue". The "boot" in the UK means a "trunk" in the USA. In the USA, a "boot" could also be is a piece of footwear. Again, it is important to know these regional differences for effective communication or you may end up getting a ride when you're trying to get in line for the elevator.

When I first met my new manager in Moscow, she wanted to take me to an authentic Ukrainian restaurant. We were having a great time and then I needed to use the restroom. Even though I could not speak Russian, I knew I could find the restroom. I proceeded to get up and almost walk right into the waiter, when I asked, "Restroom???" and pointed forward. I could tell that he did not understand me so I went on my way to find the restroom successfully. On my return to the table, I saw that my new manager is signing the check. I had thought that we were having a good time so I had a perplexed look on my face as to why she wanted to leave so suddenly. Thank goodness, I had that puzzled look on my face as she said to me, "Well, you told the waiter you wanted to leave, didn't you???" I replied, "No, I was just asking where the restroom was and he must have misunderstood thinking I was telling him I wanted to leave." Sorting out the communication, turned out to be very important in a business situation, in meeting a person for the first time and it also brought us closer together as friends. I have discovered it's important in life and business to be willing to sort through the confusion and misunderstandings.

I frequently work out of my home and one time needed to do a demonstration of my computer software for a customer in San Francisco so I thought it might be a good idea to select the lobby of (a very upscale hotel) the "W Hotel" in San Francisco. I dressed very professionally in a tailored suit with a silk blouse and high heeled shoes. The demonstration went very well and when I was finished, the prospective customer looked at his watch and said, "It's about five pm, would you like to go across the street to the topless bar???" I quickly reassessed what I was wearing to see what kind of vibe I was giving off and if one of my buttons on my blouse was unbuttoned. But no, that was not the case. So, I decided that I didn't care if I got the deal or not as a comment like that was uncalled for.

So, I said to him, "Did you just ask me to go across the street to a topless bar???" He had an incredulous look on his face, bellowed the biggest laugh and then said to me, "I didn't ask you to go to a topless bar but a tapas bar. Tapas refers to appetizers that are served in a Spanish restaurant." I had never heard of a tapas bar before but was very relieved that he was not asking me to go to a topless bar, after all. He later called his wife to join us. Again, remembering to stop, pause and ask for clarification saved a great business relationship and actually ended up creating an even greater connection than we would have had without the misunderstanding.

Being Misunderstood:

I was speaking with a co-worker, Lorraine, as we had an opportunity to get a bunch of white shirts with the company logo. I walked over to the table with Lorraine to show her the shirts and she said, "I don't wear colored shirts." I looked at the table of shirts and clearly, they were all white shirts with a red logo so I thought I would try again and said to Lorraine as I am holding the shirt, "Lorraine, you should take one of these shirts." She responded again saying, "I don't wear colored shirts." I was dumbfounded as I could not understand. Are my eyes deceiving me??? So, I tried one last time and she gave me the same reply. Come to find out she was saying that she did not wear "collared" shirts and I thought she kept saying "colored" shirts. We both had a good laugh!!! Again, if something doesn't make sense…remember to stop and ask again and truly listen to the answer.

TIP: Enunciate, Enunciate….and listen.

Another time I was at a bar that was very noisy and you could hardly hear yourself talk. To make matters worse, my friend had a very thick Scottish accent and I had a very thick Boston accent. We figured out the only good means of communication was to write each other notes on napkins. Later, we found out that the people around us thought we were deaf…. but we found a great way to build a bridge of communication that worked in that environment.

TIP: Napkins can be a very good mode of communication.

I once did a presentation for a large group of people at a conference and used the word "groovy" in my speech. Later that day, a young man very earnestly pulled me aside to clue me in to the fact that the word "groovy" had gone out of style. I could see in his face that he very earnestly wanted me to know this so I would not continue to embarrass myself by using this term. I thought this to be so sweet of him to give me the "heads up". Because I knew his intention, I thanked him profusely but it really took all that I had to not break out in laughter, as of course, I knew this term had gone out of style but I just like saying it. Remember to be gracious when others with good intentions are willing to "help you."

TIP: *Even if a word has gone out of style, if you like it, use it.*

Chapter 2
Growing Up Gross —The Early Years

Here are some lessons I discovered during those formative years that have served me well in life and business.

Captured On Video:

My father was a pioneer as he purchased an 8mm camera so my whole life has been documented from Day One. It may have been silent film but he started filming me literally while I was coming home from the hospital in my mother's arms. My father was walking backwards filming the whole event.

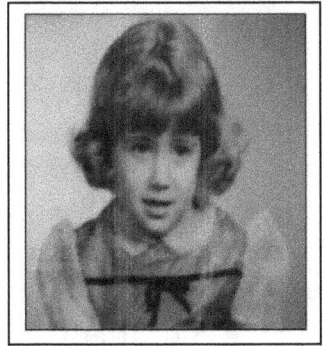

A lot of these videos have now become part of my memory as I was too young in some films for it to me my own memory. I would recommend to anyone that has children to keep a video record as it is priceless!!! My father would have us put on skits and now that we are older, we can watch these films together as a family and still get a big kick out of them. I like to say I entered the world ready to take center stage. ☺

One year my father bought boxing gloves for my two older brothers and said, "Action". So, the boys start boxing and then I get pushed in the scene for a joke. My brother was giving me a fake punch when it hit me in the eye by accident at the ripe old age of five. Sometimes we step into other people's scenes. We need to remember when it's our turn to shine and share the stage of life.

Early Television:

In our area of Boston, when I was about five years old, we watched the Bozo Show every morning. He was a funny clown. One day my mother took me to be a participant in the audience. I was so excited to have the opportunity to be on television. Before the show, they had a man tell us the rules. He said, "When I raise my hand, you need to clap as loud as you can and when I make the gesture of stomping my feet, I want you to stomp your feet as loud as you can and when I show you a stop sign, I want you to be silent. While he was giving us these rules, he was actually yelling very loudly and he was very scary. He also threatened that if we did not do what he said, we would not get the cookies they promised us. So, in the end, after the show, most of the children went crying to their parents. Things that you don't know that go on behind the scenes in television. On screen, everything seemed to be very fun but in reality, it was terrifying!!! Maybe, this is why to this day, I don't care for clowns. I learned that what goes on behind the scenes can be a very different experience then what we see on the outside. Remember to take a deeper look at things both behind the scenes and what you are being presented with to make sure you are truly getting what you are looking for.

TIP: Be leery of attending clown shows.

When I was little, before I was able to go to school, I would watch some commercials and really get influenced by them. One commercial was about oatmeal. It was called Maypo. The commercial had a little cartoon character kid sitting at the table and screaming, "I want my Maypo!!!" One time when shopping with my mother at the supermarket, I told her that I wanted Maypo. She told me that I did not like oatmeal and I told her that I thought I would like Maypo so she bought it for me. The day came when she was making my Maypo and as she was making it, I am now acting as the character on the commercial yelling, "I want my Maypo, I want my Maypo!!!" It is now time, she put the Maypo in front of me and I am now so excited to taste it. I take a big spoonful and I did not even want to swallow it as I did not like it.

TIP: *My mother is always right.*

Another commercial that I became fascinated by was for Sunbeam bread. They showed a piece of bread on screen and that it was so fresh, you did not have to cut it with a knife as by pulling at the two sides of the bread, it would amazingly cut by itself in to two even pieces. So, on another shopping trip with my mother, I convinced her that we should buy Sunbeam bread. I could not wait until I got home so I could do this bread cutting while the commercial was on TV. I get the bread and slice after slice, when I would pull the sides of the bread apart, it would become a ragged mess. I just could not figure it out.

TIP: *Watch out for false advertising.*

I think some of you might have asked your parents to buy cereal that you did not like but liked the toy that was inside the box. One time I asked my mother to buy a specific cereal, I knew I was not going to eat but just wanted the toy.

Once I got home, I tried to be very sneaky. I opened the box of cereal, dumped it out in the trash can and covered it up with other trash so my mother would not know. However, when my mother emptied the trash can, she saw the cereal I had wasted.

TIP: *You cannot hide anything from your mother.*

Brothers:

While I was growing up, I had to contend with my brother, Danny, who was six years older than me. He loved to make my lower lip quiver, because if he had that, he knew that tears were sure to follow and that would make his day. For instance, if I was watching a TV Show, he would just change the station to anything else just to upset me etc... Of course, that would make me cry to my mother, who would tell my father and then Danny would get yelled at for teasing me.

When I purchased my home, my brother, Danny, showed up on my doorstep after going to a hardware store and bought me every tool, nail, screw and ladder to make sure I had everything I needed. That gesture really touched my heart and I started to cry. Now that we are older, I tell him it is (good cry). Somehow, when I start crying, it still makes him laugh and that is why we have coined the phrase (good cry). Remember tears can be good or bad. Seek to bring out and share the good tears.

TIP: *Unconditional love is priceless so savor the moments.*

Crayfish and Aquariums:

I had an aquarium with a lot of tropical fish and one day I noticed that one crayfish was gone. We looked and looked for him and never found him until one day while my mother was vacuuming, I heard her scream. The little crayfish crawled all the way from the den to our living room. I don't know how he did it but it must have taken him quite a while and we did not even notice. Another time, I was saying hello to all of my fish and noticed the one I named, Pelican, was gone. Again, we could not understand what happened to him until one day I was doing a book report and since our aquarium was surrounded by encyclopedias, he must have jumped out and became a bookmark.

TIP: Make sure you cover your aquarium completely so you don't have any escapees.

Growing Up Gross:

I grew up with the last name Gross and learned many lessons as having such a last name helped me develop a great sense of humor. When I was in fourth grade, one evening at the dinner table, my father asked me what I learned in school that day. I replied that I had learned the definition of Gross. So, everyone at the table was a little nervous about what I would say but I told them that it meant twelve dozen or 144 things and everyone at the table clapped for me. Now I don't know if you ever saw the television show, "Leave It to Beaver", but Beaver had an older brother, Wally, who had a friend called Eddie that would always make trouble. After dinner, one of my older brother's friends, Frazier aka Eddie, came up to me and asked me if I wanted to learn another definition of Gross. So, of course, I said, "yes". He proceeded to tell me and I memorized it so I could make everyone proud of me at dinner the next evening. So, at dinner the next evening, my father asked me if I learned anything new and I told him that I learned another definition of Gross. So, he said, "Okay, tell us." Now, when you are in the fourth grade, you are just memorizing things as I did not really know the meaning of what I was saying; I was just saying what I was taught to me by my brother's friend and proceeded to tell my family the following. The definition of Gross is when you throw a pair of underwear against the wall and it sticks. Well, my father looks at my older brother and my brother starts to run and is shouting back to my father that he did not tell me anything. They later found out it was my brother's friend, Frazier.

TIP: Never memorize anything from your older brother's friend or a guy named Frazier.

Chapter 3
Growing Up Gross—The Pre-Teenage Years

Pachos:

My first puppy was called Pachos. Actually, I named him sergeant as he was always on "duty." However, my brother, Danny was taking Spanish at the time and said we should call him Pachos as that was Spanish for sergeant. When Pachos was a very small puppy, the rules in my house were not to let him on the bed as he wasn't potty trained yet. Being a little girl, I didn't really care for that rule and decided for one minute that I could put him on my bed so my friend Jackie and I could play with him. As soon as I did that, he became a fountain of pee and even though I put him on the floor as fast as I could, there was quite a puddle of pee on the bed. Since I could not tell my mother, Jackie and I decided that we would just get paper towels to soak up the damage. My mother was on the phone in the kitchen and so were the paper towels. Jackie and I took turns walking by my mother grabbing as many paper towels as we could. I guess it didn't occur to us to take the whole roll at one time. Anyway, as soon as my mother got off the phone, she went to check out what we were doing and rightfully so, I was reprimanded. I don't know why I ever bothered to try to cover up some of my antics as my mother always found me out. The truth always comes out.

TIP: *Do not try to walk by your mother every few minutes with a bunch of paper towels.*

When it was time to feed Pachos, we used canned dog food that really stunk. Then, a new dry dogfood came out that was both dry and moist but did not stink called "Prime Variety." It came in in beef, chicken and liver flavors. Because I did not like liver, when it came time to feed him the liver flavor, I would start jumping up and down in order to get him excited about eating liver. Once I put the food in the bowl, he would gobble it all up and I would say to him, "I gottcha". In thinking back, maybe the joke was on me as I never tasted it and each flavor probably tasted the same, it was just dyed brown for beef, yellow for chicken and dark brown for liver.

TIP: *If you really want to know if it is really liver, you will have to taste it.*

I loved my dog so much that while I had taken up knitting, I decided to make him a sweater. I worked very diligently on this sweater and was so excited when the day came to put the sweater on Pachos to see how much he loved it. He kept fighting me while I was putting it on him and once I did get it on him; he kept trying to tear it off with his teeth. I was so upset as I had made this sweater especially for him with tender loving care. Finally, I gave up as he obviously hated it and did not want to wear it so I gave it to my cousin for his dog who loved it.

TIP: *There is no accounting for taste.*

Pachos was very smart and we taught him all sorts of tricks. One of his favorite tricks would be to grab the handkerchief from my father's back pocket. There was no leash law at the time in my neighborhood so we could let Pachos out so he could frolic in the fields near our house with all of his puppy friends. Every once in a while, he would come home stinking of fish. I have come to believe that for some reason dogs like to rub themselves in dead fish. The chore of having to bathe my dog would take place in our dark cellar so it was not pleasant for either of us and I would constantly ask him if rolling in fish was worth it. We would have these serious conversations and I knew he understood everything that I was saying. Okay, maybe these conversations were a little one sided. We had a deal that he could sleep in my room if he would not wake me up until he saw my eyes open. Once my eyes opened, he could jump all over me. Talk about a wakeup call. I discovered, not everyone listens…and if they do listen, it doesn't mean they understand and agree.

TIP: Don't open your eyes until you are really ready to wake up.

I was on the telephone with one of my friends when my dog, Pachos, came into my room choking on a chicken bone. I was frantic and rushed him in to my car in order to get him to the veterinarian right away. I was also driving as fast as I could as he kept making these very loud gagging sounds that were unbelievable!!! I finally made it to the vet when I see a sign on the door saying that the office was closed for worming only. I kept pounding on the door until someone opened it. It looked like a very sedate bunch until we got there. I started banging on the doctor's office door so he could see my dog immediately as he was choking for his life.

Pachos kept running up and down the waiting room gagging loudly until finally with one last loud gag, the chicken bone popped out and flew across the room. After that happened, Pachos was fine and wagging his tail happily. Then, the doctor opened his office door to see what all the commotion was about. He was very upset that I had disturbed his whole office and said he was ready to see Pachos now. I told him that Pachos no longer needed his assistance but the doctor said he was going to see him anyway. In other words, I was going to pay for this. Pachos got a clean bill of health and I a lecture about chicken bones…and a hefty bill.

TIP: *If you can avoid it, don't go to the veterinarian on worming day as he might be in a bad mood if you disturb his waiting room.*

Alligators:

I did not have an alligator as a pet, however, I do have two alligator stories:

One day while playing golf in Florida, my ball went near a log. As I was getting closer to pick the ball up, I saw that it was not a log but an alligator.

TIP: *Make sure you look closely to make sure a log is a log.*

Another time, our family visited an alligator farm in Florida. These alligators were able to walk freely in the park so I started to get a little nervous and asked the man running the farm, "Did you just feed them and that is why they don't want to eat us???" He replied, "No, you just should not be the slowest one in your party." So, I said to my eighty-year-old uncle who I was walking with at the time, "Uncle Eddie, I am sticking with you!!!"

TIP: *When in danger of being eaten alive, make sure you have an exit strategy.*

Chapter 4
Growing Up Gross—From High School to College

Visiting College:

Danny and I

While I was still in high school, my brother, Danny, gave me an invitation to visit him in college. I thought this was great as it would be a good opportunity to meet college men. When I think back, I think a lot of things that I have done has been motivated by meeting men. I decided to bring one of my friends. Once we were in his dorm, I needed to go to the restroom and my brother asked me if he needed to show me where it was but I said I can find the restroom. I proceeded to open a stall and while I was sitting there, I looked down to see a man's hairy legs.

All of sudden, it dawned on me that I must have entered the men's room by mistake so I quickly ran out of there back to my brother's room and told him what I did. He said that he lived on a co-ed floor so I had the right place. I was used to sharing a bathroom at home but a co-ed bathroom at school was a little far out at the time for me.

TIP: *If you ever find yourself in that situation, make sure you bring a bathrobe.*

That evening we went to a bar and I was all dressed up to hopefully meet a nice college man. As I was walking through the crowd, I would look at a guy and he would have this funny look on his face. I thought to myself that I was looking pretty good so what could be the problem??? As I turned around, I saw my big brother giving a big scowl to any guy that looked at me. I really loved the fact that my brother is so protective of me but told him to get away as he was cramping my style.

TIP: *It really is not effective when trying to meet new men if you bring your brother along.*

Hair:

Have you ever tried to change something about your appearance??? During my teen years we would wear very tight hip hugger jeans with a tailored shirt tied up at the midriff exposing from the midriff area to below my belly button. Needless to say, my father was not thrilled with the outfit. But I had a problem that my other friends did not. They all had very straight long hair and I had very kinky curly hair.

I would spend hours and hours trying to make my hair straight and I could hear my father tell my mother how it was just not natural how long I spend in the bathroom doing my hair. In the end, all of my painstaking efforts were of no avail as once outside in the humidity, it would just curl up again. I could not win. Here is a picture of me with straight hair before I left for the senior prom.

TIP: If you have kinky curly hair move to California, as once I did, I did not have another bad hair day.

Wisdom Teeth:

Have you ever had to have your wisdom teeth taken out??? When I was about eighteen, my dentist told my mother that I needed to get my wisdom teeth taken out. He also recommended that instead of being an outpatient that I should check into the hospital. So, the day comes when I checked into the hospital and the first thing I needed to do is to go down to x-ray. Since I was an impatient, the staff needed to wheel me down to x-ray in a wheelchair and while I am waiting my turn in the waiting room, I could sense that people were looking at me with pity thinking I was crippled in a wheelchair. The thought came to me that I could stand up and say, "It is a miracle, I can walk again!!!" (I showed great restraint and resisted the temptation. But I still secretly wonder what their reaction would have been. ☺)

Once back in my bed, I just watched TV all evening and I was going to be woken up a five the next morning to go into surgery. Five am arrived and they put me on a stretcher and gave me a shot. This shot seemed to immobilize my muscles but I was fully conscious. They wheeled me down to wait my turn to go into the operating room. While lying there, I could hear the nurses chatter about how Dr. Nelson really tied one on last night and they were wondering if he would make it in. I was really hoping that I did not have Dr. Nelson but there was nothing I could do about it at the point. I was wheeled in and the anesthetist told me to count back from ten. All I remember is saying, "ten" and the next thing I knew, I was awakened by a nurse vacuuming my throat for blood.

Finally, I get back to my room that I am sharing with three other women and I needed to go to the restroom. They wanted me to use a bedpan, but I could not go that way. I begged them to take me down the hall to the restroom as I was still hooked up to an IV and could not move around myself. I get all the way down the hall when I faint and fall to the floor so they picked me up and put me back in bed. However, I did not get a chance to go to the bathroom so when my family arrived, I asked them to take me down the hall and the same thing happened.

I know I went in the hospital to get my wisdom teeth taken out, but by the time I arrived home I was black and blue from falling so much.

TIP: *If you can help it, don't get your wisdom teeth taken out…and if you do have to have them removed.… perhaps consider using the bedpan as they recommend.… you get fewer bruises that way.*

Attending College:

Finally, it was my turn to go to college in Western Massachusetts which was two hours west of Boston. I was leaving my nucleus of friends in Boston to experience the great unknown. It was now time to pack up the belongings that I wanted to take with me. At the same time, my parents were retiring and getting ready to move to a warmer climate. This meant they were also packing up all of their belongings as they had sold the house that I had lived in all of my life. We were going through a lot of big transitions all at once.

As my mother was packing, I saw her wrap up a napkin holder that I had made for her in ceramics class when I was about twelve. It really touched my heart that she would still want to keep such a crazy item as it was lopsided and really funny looking with black and white polka dots included finger impressions, but to this day, it is the napkin holder she has on her kitchen table. Then, I saw her pick up a vase I had made that was lopsided and I thought she really loved that piece, as well, when I saw her put it in the trash. I was mortified and exclaimed to my mother, "Ma, how can you even think of throwing that vase away!!! I thought you loved it!!!" So, I told her that I was going to take it to college with me. Just to have fun, when people would visit me, I would ask them how much they thought I had paid for the vase. Because I asked them in that manner, they would pause and then say something like $200 and I would just laugh!!! We get to choose the treasures we keep and take with us, as well as, those we elect to leave behind.

TIP: As the saying goes by Margaret Wolfe Hungerford, "Beauty is in the eye of the beholder".

Restrooms:

Yes, another restroom experience. During a trip back home from college, we stopped for food. I needed to use the restroom so I started to follow a girl with long black hair as she looked like she knew where she was going. As I entered the room, I was confronted with a bunch of men using the urinals and quickly ran out of there!!! I was not following a woman but a man!!! Make sure in life you are following the right person…that they are actually taking you were you want to go.

TIP: Long hair is not always a good indicator to figure out someone's gender.

Hair Again:

I know I already told you the problems that I had with my hair but once I went to college, my college roommate told me (since she had the same textured hair as I did) that I should get it cut short. I always wanted long straight hair that would swish back and forth but I never had that kind of hair. It didn't matter what products I put in my hair, it was always going to be curly. I was frightened of cutting it as I would not have any way to control it and make it straight with an elastic but I decided to do it. I was alone in the chair as the beautician turned me away from the mirror and proceeded to cut my hair. Once he was finished, he turned me to the mirror and I was shocked as now I had to be my curly haired self. In my shock, I proceeded outside to a very cold winter evening where I could feel the cold against my neck, something I had never experienced with long hair. As it turned out, it was the best thing I could have done and it made my life much easier. This new haircut also made me look quite different and when attending our Thanksgiving high school football game, initially old friends didn't even say hello, as they did not know who I was.

TIP: Style comes and goes so appreciate what Mother Nature has given to you.

Babysitting Adventure:

When I was about thirteen years old, I had a babysitting career for a **very short** while. I was babysitting one evening for some neighbors who had an eight-year-old daughter, Paula, and a four-year-old son, Bobby. I was watching television when I heard a drizzling sound. I looked outside and it wasn't raining so I starting to investigate where the sound was coming from. I found Bobby peeing behind the refrigerator so I quickly grabbed him and headed to the bathroom which was locked. I asked Paula to open the door so Bobby could go in. Paula, after a few seconds, opened the door of the bathroom and started rubbing something on Bobby's face. Bobby started screaming as what Paula was rubbing on him was "Ben Gay" (for those of you who don't know what Ben Gay is, it gives the sensation of burning your skin). After that ordeal, I was just trying to get them to go to sleep. They kept jumping up and down on the bed so I told them that they could only jump one more time and that is when little Bobby hit his head on the headboard. He reached back to his head and showed me blood so I just started screaming while Bobby was perfectly calm. I ran to get my mother and everything turned out okay but I retired as a babysitter.

TIP: Beware of four-year-old and eight-year-old children.

Dr. Berson:

Since the day I was born, I had the same pediatrician and he would even see me once I was in college because he knew me so well. I remember being on college break and going to see Dr. Berson. I would be waiting in the waiting room with all mothers and children and people would look at me wondering where my children were. Well, I was the child and when he would be ready to see me, I would sit on his table next to a baby scale and it would always make me laugh.

TIP: Don't get too attached to one doctor as a day will come when you must find a new one.

College Scare:

When I first arrived at college, I had not had time to meet a lot of people yet and when I went to take a shower, noticed a lump on my breast. I really didn't want to tell total strangers about it and I also did not want to worry my mother until I knew exactly what it was so I made an appointment at the college infirmary. I kept this information to myself while I waited to see the doctor. However, I also knew that when you keep things to yourself, especially worrisome issues, it just makes you more anxious and it is always best to share.

Luckily, I did not have to wait long as it was a teaching hospital so they had a lot of appointments available. However, that meant that a bunch of medical students also attended these examinations. I laid down, totally nude from the waist up with about ten medical students gazing on to watch the doctor do the examination which was not the most comfortable situation. The doctor looked closely at my breast and then exclaimed, "That is not a lump, it's a pimple!!!" Everyone had a good laugh including me!!!

TIP: In every embarrassing event there is a silver lining.

Used Car:

My parents bought me a used car to get around from college to Cape Cod. Come to find out when I arrived in Cape Cod, there was a problem with the car; it needed a new cylinder. Not having the money to do the work, I decided to live with the problem and sell the car to a mechanic once I got back to college. In the meantime, what would happen to me was that sometimes when I had to come to a complete stop, I would have to get a can of carburetor starter and spray a certain location lifting it with a screwdriver under the hood. I seemed to get by, as if I knew I was coming to a red light, I would drive so slowly that hopefully it would turn green before I got there.

I finally made it back to college and put an ad in the paper to sell the car to a mechanic, disclosing everything I knew about it and he told me that he wanted to buy it. I was very pleased and proceeded to take the spare tire and jack out of the car. He told me that the spare tire and jack go with the car. At first, I was skeptical as this was the first time I was selling a car and I wanted to make my father proud of me. I looked at him to make sure as best I could that he was telling me the truth and said, "Okay, I'm trusting you on this one as I really don't want to have to tell my father that I messed up the sale." He said, "Trust me, I'm telling you the truth and what would you do with a spare tire and a jack without a car???" It made sense so I agreed. Later, when I got back to my house, I called my father to tell him the whole story and he had a good laugh about it.

TIP: *The jack and the spare tire go with the car.*

Chapter 5
Growing up Gross—Boyfriend Dating Adventures

Regarding my first boyfriend at about age fifteen, I felt like I played the part of Olivia Newton-John in the movie, "Grease". As my four "goody two shoes" friends and I were attracted to the bad boys and the leader of the pack was Tony, who played John Travolta. We didn't do bad things; we were just so attracted to them as we thought they were so cool. Our parents were terrified but they knew if we stayed together, we would be safe. The boys were good with their hands (no pun intended) and built a clubhouse in a field near Tony's house. We had electricity with black lights and music. It was so cool!!!

On Halloween, Tony decided to just fool around and started wrapping black crepe paper around my face while we were decorating the clubhouse as we were just being silly and everyone was having a good time. Then, I realized it was getting late and time to go home as we had a curfew of nine pm I opened the door to my house, walked into the kitchen and my mother asked what was wrong with my face. I couldn't understand what she was talking about, but when I looked in the mirror, I realized my boyfriend had been wrapping black crepe paper around my head and the black dye was left on my face leaving me with a dark splotchy face. My mother was not too thrilled that I was dating this boy so I had to quickly come up with an excuse.

I told her that I was doing cartwheels with my friends and landed in a pile of dust. I have to admit, that had to be the lamest excuse I ever gave (I think). Did my mother really believe that story??? I don't think so but she trusted me enough not want to go into any more detail.

TIP: If you are not a good liar then don't even try. I think it is easier to tell the truth as embarrassing as it might seem at the time.

BONUS TIP: Always check the mirror before making an entrance. Tis wise to make sure your reflection truly matches who you are and what you want to bring to the world.

Brother's Friend:

When I was about sixteen, I had a crush on Brian, a younger brother of one of my brother's friends. It was my belief that my brother really didn't want me associating with him, because if he had to defend my honor in some way, it could cause problems with his friendship with Brian and his brother. However, I confided in my mother that I wanted to date Brian. A couple of days later, I received a telephone call from Brian asking me out so I figured my mother said something to my brother so Brian would call me. Since I thought Brian was told to call, I refused to go out with him. When Danny found out about this, he was laughing like crazy as he said he had nothing to do with it. Now, I didn't know what to do so I called Brian back and apologized and we decided to have dinner.

On the evening of the date, it was just as though my brother, Danny, was on the date with us as he seemed to be the most comfortable topic of discussion. At dinner, I had ordered Chicken Kiev. When the waitress came to our table to place the chicken in front of me, she asked, "Do you know how to eat this???" I was horrified that on my first date, the waitress was asking me if I knew how to eat chicken. I am thinking, "Is she crazy???" I had an incredulous look on my face so she finally added, "The reason I am asking if you know how to eat this is because if you have never had Chicken Kiev before, you have to be really careful on how you place the knife into the chicken so it doesn't spat in your eye as it is baked with butter and other stuff." Needless to say, the whole date was a fiasco and that was the end of my love affair with Brian.

TIP: Sometimes it is not meant to be and you just have to let it go. On the bright side, I discovered how to properly eat Chicken Kiev which I have been able to do on other dates.

Limousines:

I once had a boyfriend who drove a limousine and one time in between gigs, he called me up to take me for a ride and surprised me with a dozen roses. I was thrilled and as we drove around decided to pick up one of my friends to ride along with us. We picked her up and I was sitting in the front seat with my boyfriend who's driving and she is sitting in the back. We had the partition down so we could talk, and all of a sudden, my friend starts playing with the buttons and the partition comes up cutting all of my roses at the top of the stems where the roses fall off and all I am left holding is a bouquet of stems.

TIP: *Partitions have consequences.*

Halloween: I was asked by a new boyfriend to go out one Halloween to a party but before the party to go the San Diego Padres baseball game. That morning, I clumsily dropped a half gallon bottle of grapefruit juice on my toe. It hurt a lot and my toe did swell a little but I was still going to go out and dressed extravagantly for the occasion. He was supposed to be wearing a gorilla suit. When I opened my door to let him in, he was wearing a Hawaiian shirt and jeans. Needless to say, the only one dressed up that night at the baseball game was me and the San Diego Chicken (their mascot).

Another Halloween, I had the occasion to be Dracula's date.

Surprise:

As we know, dating can be very interesting, embarrassing, etc...

I once met a man who looked like he had a full head of hair. On our third date, we started kissing on my sofa and I put my hand in his hair. I felt something like Velcro and asked what it was and all of a sudden, he whipped the wig off and threw it to the floor. I was totally shocked!!! He was totally bald. It would be one thing if I knew he was bald but to be in the midst of a romantic kiss and to suddenly see your amour a few minutes ago with a full head of hair and then totally bald really threw me for a loop!!! The romantic moment was lost. Every time I looked at the spot on the rug where he threw his wig, it always reminded me of him.

TIP: *You really don't want to be remembered when someone looks at a spot on their floor.*

Capitola:

On a first date with another Tony, it was decided to spend the day in Capitola. It was a lovely day so we strolled the beach for two hours. Then, he suggested that we have a drink at a restaurant high upon a hill nearby. When we got to the restaurant, it was very romantic. There was a gondola that took you down to the main entrance. Once inside, it was just beautiful with a waterfall and a fireplace. We were finishing our drinks when he asked where I would like to have dinner so I suggested, "Let's stay here." He was fine with that but told me that he had to put more money in the meter as the car had been parked in public parking for about two hours already.

Since the drive to Capitola is about an hour from where we live and since we obviously didn't know each other that well, he offered to leave his car keys with me so I would be assured that he wasn't going to drive away. I told him to take his keys as I trusted him and I also told him that by the time he gets back I will have found us a table as it was first come first serve. There was a full glass of wine in front of me at the bar as he left. As I turned to see where we could find a table, I accidentally hit the glass of wine; it fell on my ankle and crashed to the floor. The bartender and waitresses quickly cleaned the mess up and I was so grateful that everything was exactly the way it was before he left except for one ankle of my black pants being soaked with wine. I thought, great, he will never know about the wine spillage.

Once he returned, he innocently grabbed my soaked ankle and he didn't say anything and I didn't say anything, as well, for the longest time. Finally, he started to slowly move his hand up my leg to feel when the wetness might stop... He said, "Did you spill your wine???" I said, "Yes." He said, "Did the wine glass break on the floor???" I said, "Yes." He said, "Thank Goodness, as the only other thing I could think of was that you stuck your foot in the toilet bowl." Now, isn't that romantic.

TIP: Even if you do spill wine on your black pants, keep smiling. It will all workout.

Chapter 6
The Ultimate Sportswoman

Have you ever been invited to participate in a sport that you were not familiar??? I have many times. Here are some of my experiences. As a side note…. if you were to look at me, the first thought that would come to mind would not be the ultimate sportswoman but I have a few stories to share that you might have experienced, as well.

Water Skiing:

While at camp, I took my first lesson on how to water ski. I was told to bend my knees and hold on to the tow and when the boat goes, you just go with it. I was ready, the boat pulled me up and they thought I was doing so well that they started weaving me in and out of the wake. That frightened me so I fell in the water and held on to the tow for dear life as I didn't want them to leave me in the middle of the lake. They kept dragging and dragging me through the water and I was saying to myself, why don't they stop the boat??? I kept taking in more and more water until I could not take it anymore and finally let go of the tow. They then came to me and started yelling at me asking why I did not let go the tow sooner. They then informed me, that if they had stopped the boat while I was still holding on to the tow, I would have been pulled into the motor.

A lesson I took from this, is it's important to know what to do if things don't go according to plan and you fall down. There is a time to let go.

TIP: If you fall while water skiing, let go of the tow.

Diving:

Once day my brother decided he would teach me how to dive. Since he is my older brother and feels responsible for me, teaching me how to dive became a very serious matter instead of the fun thing that I thought it would be. By the time, we got to the lake with all the diving gear, I was in tears as he kept telling me that I had to listen to him and not fool around. I couldn't put on my mask because of all my tears. I knew in my heart he was just worried about my safety but I didn't feel much like having a diving class at that point. A little boy watching the interaction between my brother and I said, "Hey, if you're not using the mask, can I???" We both stopped and laughed. Remember to let learning something new still be fun and allow someone else to lighten the mood and shift the focus when needed.

TIP: If you are not using your diving gear, share with others.

Snow Skiing:

While at college, some of my friends wanted to go skiing and I was the only one who did not know how to ski. They told me that I could just go on the "bunny hill" and it would be fine. So, I did. However, the boots that you wear are such clodhoppers and clunky; very hard to move around. Also, I was nervous about just jumping off the ski lift as I did not consider this a little "bunny hill" as it looked like a mountain to me!!! Once in position at the top of the mountain, they just told me to go. So, off I go and I am going so fast that I throw myself down. They all came around me to pick me up and said that I did such a great job. I told them that I did not know how to slow myself down and that is when they told me if I wanted to slow myself down to do a "snowplough". I asked them, "Why did you not tell me about "snowploughing" before???" They replied that they wanted me to get over my fear of failing (falling). Well, after that, I told them to go on their way to the bigger mountain and I would keep practicing by myself. I felt that the hardest part of skiing was getting up once you fell. Luckily for me, there was a ski team practicing and they took turns picking me up. After a while, I decided to take a break and went to the lodge to get some coffee. As I came out of the lodge with my cup of coffee to watch the skiers, I tripped on a stair and fell as the coffee flew up out of my hand and then all over me and my fantastic outfit. I don't know if this has ever happened to you before, but sometimes you get so embarrassed once you fall that you don't move and look around to see if anyone saw you. Trust me, people always see you.

**ized*TIP: Beware of steps if you are wearing clodhopper clunky ski boots.*

Cross Country Skiing:

I had an opportunity to take a cross country skiing class at Amherst College. *(Okay, once again my motivation was to meet men.)* I wasn't sure how to do this type of skiing but decided to try and learn. I thought it would be easy but you are still in those clodhopper clunky boots and even though the terrain was not as scary as downhill skiing, it took hours of strenuous trudging in the snow. What I won't do in the name of love.

TIP: Cross country skiing does not enhance your love life.

Softball:

I've tried softball and I don't care what you say, it is not a soft ball as it feels like a very hard ball to me. I don't want to catch these not softballs as I do not want to break my nails. I was given a position behind the pitcher so I thought I would be safe so someone else could catch it. Every time the bat hit the ball, it was as if it was coming right at me like a heat seeking missile. I think the real reason is that everyone knew on the other team that I was not really excited to be catching the ball as whenever it came at me either the pitcher, first baseman, second baseman or third baseman would run to try to catch it. They had figured out my secret and now I was a liability. So, I decided, okay, the next ball that comes my way, I am going for it. As it happens, the ball comes at me and I am running while looking up in order to catch the ball. I hear the crowd cheering and I am thinking they are applauding my efforts as I ran right into the back of the pitcher with full force and fell. Well, I didn't catch the ball but at least I got a standing ovation for trying (and I didn't break a nail)!!!

TIP: It is not how you play the game but give it your best and try.

Basketball:

I once went to Seattle on business and was invited to see a basketball game. It seemed to me that they were constantly mopping up the floor and I turned to my boss to ask him if the game was being televised. He said, "No" and asked me why I'm asking this question. I said, "Well, since they are mopping up the floor so frequently, I thought they were worried about sneaker marks for the TV viewing audience."

My boss said back laughingly, "They're not worried about sneaker marks, they're mopping up sweat." I then felt a little sick to my stomach thinking about how some people in the first row might be splashed with sweat considering how frequently they must mop up.

TIP: *If I were you, I would not sit in the front row of any basketball game.*

Tubing:

My company had an event at a Ski Resort in Maine for all employees which included participating in several activities. I showed up wearing my jeans, a fashionable ski sweater, high heeled black boots and velvet gloves with my beret, of course. Everyone was giving me a hard time for what I was wearing, especially for the high heeled boots, as I am not known among my friends and family as being a big sports participant. However, since everyone was participating, I decided to also fully participate.

One of the activities was snow tubing down a mountain in a rubber inner tube. The way it worked was that you would lay face down placing your stomach in the center of the inner tube. Then, you would push yourself down the mountain. There was going to be an award for the fastest men's and women's time down the course. Please note, I love awards…but, going for the fastest downhill time didn't sound worth it to me.

I was so afraid to push myself off that someone had to push me and I went flying down the course. I was screaming at the top of my lungs, frightened that I would bang myself up against the side of the course and that would be the end of me. As it turned out, I made the fastest women's time on the course and I believe it was all due to the aerodynamic capabilities that my high heel boots provided.

TIP: Don't let others discourage you about your wardrobe…Embrace your Fabulousness!!!

Horseback Riding:

I took horseback riding lessons when I was a little girl and these horses weren't taken care of very well!!! I think they were also very old as they walked very slowly but that was a good speed for me as I really did not know what I was doing. They might have been old but they were smart as once they started the trail, they would walk very close to the tree trunks. You see that if you are on a horse and they start walking close to the tree trunks, the rider is going to get hit with branches and get scratched up which is what happened to me. During the trail, we came upon a very shallow pond. Well, my horse decided that he did not feel like crossing the pond that day and started to get down on his knees. He not only got on his knees but then started to roll over. I think his back was itchy as I do not think they groomed these horses very well. I quickly jumped off or I would have been a pancake. I guess the horse was in charge and not me.

My next opportunity was to go horseback riding on the beach. I was told to wear sneakers but it was such a hot day, I decided to wear flip flops. When it was time to select your horse, I put in a special request for my horse to have arthritis as I was not a very confident rider so they gave me a horse they said would suit my needs. Once on the trail, walking very slowly on the beach, there was a loud bang and my horse took off running and my flip flops flew off. I was screaming as there was no way I was going to be able to control this horse. Thankfully, the guy who was in charge of the operation caught up with me and stopped my horse, otherwise, I think I would still be riding into the sunset. I accepted that perhaps horses are not my thing.

TIP: Never trust horses, wear correct shoes and ask/scream for help when needed.

Kayaking:

My company would have annual trips for their Sales Reps who exceeded their goals called President's Club. I love achieving my goals. One time, we were in Puerto Rico at the Hyatt Resort.

One of the team building exercises we were asked to do was kayak racing. I had never done any kayaking before but the lifeguard gave the group a three-minute lesson. It was to be a race on who would have the fastest time on the obstacle course that they created for us in the ocean.

Okay, we were off and I seemed to be doing quite well, at first. Then, when it was time to turn around to go back to shore, I was unable to turn my kayak around and was going out to sea. Everyone from the shore was calling me to come back (as though I didn't know I was going the wrong way). Finally, the lifeguard came for me and helped turn me around.

I thought, okay, that was over with. However, they wanted us to do the course one more time. This time I didn't go out to sea but had a tough time getting around one particular buoy. Again, the lifeguard had to help turn me around. I discovered it's important to know how to turn around in kayaking just as it is in life.

A lot of people in my company thought I had trouble on purpose in order to get to know the lifeguard better as he was pretty cute. At the end of the week, my company gave us all a gag gift and mine was a postcard with a picture of a very cute guy (like the lifeguard) asking me to meet him at his cabana at nine pm.

TIP: Pretending you are not good at kayaking is definitely a good way to meet a lifeguard.

Tennis:

I really love to play tennis. However, it is one sport that is not easy to play by yourself unless you buy a tennis ball machine. So that is exactly what I did.

Before I bought it, however, I wanted to get some idea on how heavy it was as I was not sure what thirty pounds would feel like. They told me it was like lifting a small TV so I thought I could handle that. Well, when I first picked it up, it seemed to weigh a lot more than a small TV but I managed. I charged it up according to the instructions and was all ready to play the next day.

On its first play day, it was difficult to find a court as it was a very busy Sunday but I managed to get one next to four guys. I set it up per directions, filled it up with about fifty balls, turned it on and ran to the other side of the court so I could start hitting the balls the machine was sending to me. I guess I didn't set it up quite right as the balls started shooting up over to the next court showering total strangers with balls. I ran as quickly as I could to turn the machine off and then proceeded to reset it so the balls wouldn't come out so high. When I turned the machine back on, I quickly ran to the other side of the court to be ready to hit the balls.

To my dismay, the balls were now just dribbling out of the machine so I had obviously overcompensated on my new settings.

I could see across the way that the court with the four guys playing beside me were getting a great kick out of this comedy show I was providing for them. It took a while before I finally got the settings right but then I finally did it. I turned it on and ran across the court so I could start hitting the balls. I think I really set it appropriately this time as it was sending the balls and also oscillating back and forth just as if I was playing against a real player. Unfortunately, with all the time I took in adjusting the settings, the ball machine ran out of juice so I ended up having to go home before I really played at all.

I did try playing with the machine after that now that I had the correct settings. Families would come walking by and the kids would ask their parents to buy them one. I was almost tempted to sell it but thought I would get good use out of it.

Needless to say, there is no substitute for a real person. When you make a commitment to meet someone for a tennis game, you have to show up or the other person would get upset that you cancelled your plans. It's that added incentive to get out and go. The biggest problem I had with the tennis ball machine was that if I made a date to play tennis with it and I later cancelled because I got lazy, the tennis ball machine didn't feel bad or anything??? I needed the added feature of instilling guilt.

TIP: There is no substitute for a person even when you have a well running tennis ball machine.

Chapter 7
First Jobs

Do you remember your first jobs??? The learning curve, the excitement, and the challenges??? Here are a couple of stories from some of my First Jobs.

My first job was with Dunkin Donuts at the ripe old age of fourteen years old.

I started as a waitress but was so good that I was promoted to filler. I really got into my work especially when I had to get the jelly and lemon etc... out of the vats and into the pumps for donut filling. My boss always told me to take my jewelry off before working on the donuts, however, I didn't listen to that rule very well.

One Sunday, after my shift, my boss said that he had to go to the bank. I was ready to clean up when I looked at my hands and saw that my ring was on my finger but the emerald stone was gone!!! I quickly started to pull back all of the donuts I filled that morning and started ripping them up to try to find my emerald. My boss came back to find me ripping up all of his profits and screamed, "What are you doing???" I told him that I was looking for my emerald so we both watched from the big window where you would see the baker rolling the dough as to whether someone would swallow my emerald or he would be hit with a lawsuit for someone breaking a tooth on it. In any case, whatever happened to my emerald, I will never know as no one ever reported anything. So, either it was swallowed and passed through or the doughnut was thrown away.

TIP: Next time, listen to your boss when he might have more experience than you regarding a certain activity.

Pollster:

I had a great job for a short time before I went to college working for a State Senator in Massachusetts.

Polling can be very tedious as you are usually working from a script so I thought I needed to make this exercise fun for me. We were calling every eighth name in the phone book in his district. So, if I was calling Susan Stone, I would say, "Hello, my name is Susan Stone" in order to see if the person I was calling was even paying attention to what I was saying as it appeared I had the same name as they did. Some thought it a very funny coincidence and some didn't pick up on the fact that I had the same name as them at all. Oh well, it made it more fun for me to do the poll, as well as, for others in the group.

TIP: Try to make every activity fun for you.

Summer Jobs

Enjoy some of my Summer Job Adventures.

Camp Counselor:

Once my parents moved to California and I was living away at college, I needed a job where I could also live during the summer. I elected to be a camp counselor in Maine. I bought a new bathing suit for the occasion. Since I was late in making my decision for this job, by the time I got to camp, all of the other counselors had a chance to get to know each other. When I arrived, it was third period swimming. I had my new bathing suit on and once the waterfront director saw me, he said that I had to get into the water to show him that I could swim and tread water in order to be able to stand on the dock. He purposely made me tread water for a lengthy time but I didn't care as I was a great swimmer.

Once I passed my test, I got out of the water and everyone was really friendly in introducing themselves to me, especially the guys. I thought it rather odd that as people were saying hello to me on the dock, they were looking at my body instead of my face. After third period swimming was over, it was time to go back to the bunk where I then saw myself in the full-length mirror. I was just horrified as my bathing suit was totally see-through!!! I guess once the white bathing suit got wet, it left nothing to the imagination. I asked another counselor once we returned back to the bunk why she didn't mention anything to me and she said, "Well, after all it is YOUR bathing suit!!!"

TIP: Beware of white bathing suits when wet.

I thought even though I was a counselor, I was going to be able to participate in all sorts of sports and learn how to do better at archery, ceramics, skiing… Well, no, as the criteria to be the boating instructor at this camp was that I could swim??? I would take eight children at a time in a row boat and instead of wanting to learn how to row, they seemed to want to tip the boat over. I knew I could swim but I didn't know how well they could swim. So, I had to think of something to keep their attention and thought of the idea that we would sing songs and that worked!!!

TIP: Even if you don't have a great voice, singing can be inspirational.

Even though the camp was located deep in the woods, we would do overnights sleeping in a tent. On one occasion, while we were sleeping in tents, a bee stung me in the eye. I did not feel much physical pain but my eye swelled up so much that I looked like a one-eyed monster. To make matters worse, there was a social at a boy's camp the next day where we would be introduced to new people. Talk about making a great first impression.

TIP: Remember to always smile as being a one-eyed monster for a day or two can be a great conversation starter.

Peer Group Pressure:

Initially, I did not like the Waterfront Director as I thought he was somewhat arrogant and he did not really mingle with the rest of the counselors and seemed quite aloof. We only had one night off each month and the night he was off, all of the counselors (including me as a prank) took very large wooden benches that could only be lifted by at least two people and barricade the entrance to his bunk so he would have to sleep outside once he came back to camp. Everyone was laughing as we did this but as each bench was leveled higher and higher against his door, I started feeling worse and worse and rather disgusted with everyone including myself. So, what I decided to do was wait in front of his bunk until he got back from his day off. As he approached the bunk, I could see that he was so upset and he had no clue of what to do but then he saw me. We both, one by one, took the benches down so he could get in his room and we both had tears in our eyes. I then got a chance to really know him and he later became my boyfriend. ☺

TIP: Do not conform to peer group pressure and just follow a pack. Be yourself and stand up for what you believe in. When I think of that story, it always makes me stronger. (Remember to stand in your truth and don't just follow the crowd.... but follow your heart.)

Waitress:

For another summer job, I decided to rent a house with a group of people in Cape Cod, Massachusetts. We knew we were qualified to either pump gas or wait on tables. I knew I was not pumping gas so I applied at a rock and roll club called "Rascals" in Yarmouth. They hired fourteen girls and only planned on keeping seven of us. Even though it was a rock and roll club, the year I worked there, they decided to have a "Roaring Twenties" image. So, I had to wear a red dress with long white pearls and black high heeled shoes. The bouncers and bartenders had to wear tuxedos. Unusual for the cape, but oh well...

Every evening before my shift, I would go to the Dunkin Donuts and the older people would immediately start whispering about me thinking I might be a prostitute by the "Roaring Twenties" clothing I was wearing. There were certain rules I had to adhere to while serving drinks at "Rascals". No trays on the table when serving drinks and never write any order down on a napkin. One time I brought two guys, two rum and cokes. When I delivered the drinks...They said, "We didn't order these, we ordered two gin and tonics." I apologized and said, "I'm really sorry but can you drink them, I'm new." Not only did they drink the drinks but they got such a kick out of my response that I got a great tip. By the end of the summer, I got pretty good. I could hold a pitcher of beer in one hand and a tray of drinks in the other. It was so loud in the club, they would never hear me when I said, "Excuse me." So, I would just kick them in the ankle so that I might get through the crowd.

I promised my mother that I would call her in California every night so she would know her baby (me) was all right. We didn't own a phone so the closest phone was at a phone booth at the State Police Station. I would get into the phone booth and once I would shut the door, the booth would light up. All the police cruisers would come driving by and I told my mother that I better get off the phone quickly as they might think I was a prostitute because of the looks of my clothing.

TIP: Even if you make a mistake, try to use it to your advantage and either learn from it or laugh!!!

I Just Had To Do It!!!

A vodka company was promoting their logo on some sponges. These sponges were very stiff, thin and flat but once you submerged them in water, they became an average sponge that you would normally find at your local supermarket. I didn't get too many days off from "Rascals" but one night I went to another bar with friends and I happened to still have some sponges in my purse when I went out that evening. I took a seat at the bar next to a stranger and ordered a drink. After I paid for my drink, my purse was left slightly opened and I noticed from the corner of my eye that this stranger was eyeing my sponges. I quickly moved the sponges back into my purse and said to him... "Oh, how embarrassing!!! You weren't supposed to see those!!!" He said, "Why not??? What are they???" I said, "Well, I try to keep this a secret but I am on a new diet program that provides these sponges. All I have to do is tear off a corner of one before every meal and drink some water. I have been doing it for about a week and have lost a lot of weight." I then started carrying on a conversation with my friends around me and out of the corner of my eye, I saw this guy trying to take one of the sponges from me. I stopped him just in time!!! I couldn't believe that he took me seriously. Can you imagine that headline, "Man dies of ingesting sponges!!!"

TIP: *Beware when you hear about really crazy diets.*

Smoking Etiquette:

I started smoking cigarettes when I was about seventeen with my friends. We would take turns at whose house to use when our parents weren't home to practice how to inhale. One time, my friend, Jackie and I had an opportunity to practice how to inhale but we didn't have any cigarettes. However, I found one of my father's cigars and thought that would be good enough. (Who knew that you weren't supposed to inhale cigars???)

As it so happened, my parents came home earlier than expected so I had to think of something quick to get the smell of smoke out of the bathroom. Aha, I knew exactly what to do. I got an orange, peeled it and then started rubbing the orange peels on the walls of the bathroom. The room totally smelled like oranges and I knew that I would be totally in the clear.

I went to my room and later there was a knock on the door from my mother. She had a perplexed look on her face and said, "I have one question for you, Barbara. Why were you eating oranges in the bathroom???" You know, she got me again as I just didn't have an answer for that. Busted again!!!

TIP: *Don't even think about trying to lie to your Mother.*

I started a new job and had a business meeting on the 40th floor of the Sears Tower in Chicago to meet an entirely new group of people that I would be working with. It was the dead of winter but I wanted to have a cigarette during a short break. I had the option of taking the elevator all the way down to the lobby or better yet, I came up with a new idea. I will go in the fire stairwell. Once I opened the door and heard it click behind me, I knew I was in trouble just by the sound. I was now locked in the stairwell. Even though I was screaming at the top of my lungs for someone to let me out, no one opened the door. I soon came to the realization that I might have to walk down forty stories but I kept up my screaming.

Finally, my boss opened the door and asked me what I was doing in the stairwell. Once I told him, he started to laugh as he said as he was walking by; all he could hear were little quiet yelps of "Help, Help etc..." They must have really done a great job in soundproofing that building.

TIP: Never go in the stairwell if you plan to enter back in the building the same way without a key.

New York and Cigarettes:

One time I was visiting my cousin in New York City and she had ordered some food from a restaurant across the street. I told her that I could pick it up (so in the meantime) I could have a cigarette. As soon as I got outside, ready to cross the street to the restaurant, a crowd of men circled me in a very intimidating manner. Inwardly, I was very frightened but outwardly, I gave them a look not to mess with me. Finally, they just asked me for a cigarette and let me go across the street to the restaurant where I immediately called my cousin to send her husband over to rescue me.

TIP: Don't smoke as it is hazardous to your health.

Chapter 8
Things Happen For A Reason

I am not that in to poetry but I love the poem by Robert Frost, *"The Road Not Taken"*.

"Two roads diverged in a wood, and I — I took the one less traveled by and that has made all the difference."

I believe that if I did not do that last thing, I would have never been qualified for the next thing. Even though I had a love for psychology, my mother told me to get my degree in Education as you can always fall back on being a teacher. Since, I always listen to my mother that is what I did as she has always been right. I stated previously, once I graduated from college, it was time to visit La Jolla and as it turned out, I loved it and decided to call it home. When I started to look for a teaching position, I was told that there were so many teachers coming to California for a job that I had to get a fifth year of college first.

So, I decided to enroll in classes to get my Master's in Psychology. I was able to go to school full time for a while as I had saved some money but then had to find job that would let me leave at three thirty pm on Tuesdays and Thursdays so I could finish up school while still making money. I went on several interviews but the interview I am about to describe was one of the craziest. However, it put me on a new career path that was totally unexpected and highly rewarding.

TIP: Always listen to my mother as she will always have your best interest at heart.

Interview Preparation:

I wanted to make sure that I was looking my best so I bought a very nice suit and I needed the perfect white high heeled shoes to match. I searched and finally found the style I really liked. Unfortunately, one of the shoes that had an elastic band at the top to hold the toes together was damaged. Well, I thought to myself that I could take these shoes to a shoemaker and he could fix the elastic in the toe, which he was able to do. I was so happy and prepared for the interview.

TIP: If something is defective before purchase, it will be defective after purchase.

Interview Day:

I made sure that I would arrive early and I thought I was looking good when suddenly, the elastic on my shoe pops!!! Oh no, how will I even be able to walk up the stairs to my interview??? I had to think quickly and the idea came to me. I asked the receptionist for a stapler so I could staple the shoe where the elastic broke. Emergency avoided and I was able to walk up the steps to start my interview. As Maggie, the interviewer, started to ask me questions, I felt that she was looking at my shoe so I told her what had happened in the lobby and that I stapled it. She then had a very perplexed look on her face but continued asking me questions.

I then felt that she was staring at my hair. At that time, I did not dry my hair but let it dry naturally. I thought to myself, she does not know me and maybe she thinks that I haven't washed my hair in years so I just felt compelled to tell her that I felt she was staring at my hair and I wanted her to know it was wet. After I made that comment, she now had another funny look on her face. I thought to myself, after this interview, I will never get this job but Maggie walked me to the door and told me that she would be in contact with me if I was selected for the position. Sure, enough, my phone rang and I got the job. I was so stunned!!! It was only years later, once I got to know Maggie really well, that I asked her, "That interview was so bizarre, why on earth would you hire me and she replied, "Exactly, you were so bizarre, I knew you would fit right in!!!

TIP: Even though you think the interview is going terribly wrong, keep going as you may be surprised by the results.

A Job Opportunity That Changed My Life:

I interviewed for this job just to help make money to pay for school but what I found was a brand-new career path that I had not imagined. I did like teaching children but what I did not like was to make them stay after school or giving any kind of reprimand. This was a job to work in the computer industry where I would learn new technology and then teach it to adults whose companies were paying for them to attend and pay attention. I was constantly learning new things and then teaching others. I was very happy in that position and I was so successful in teaching, training and doing demos for the sales reps that I was later asked to go into a sales position. That sounded frightening to me but my boss saw something in me that I didn't see in myself and offered me the security that if I did not like sales, I could still have my former job back. As it turned out, I was very successful and like to mentor others when given the opportunity.

TIP: Be open of possible new doors that may open exciting opportunities for you that you would never have imagined.

Computer Terminology:

When working with computers, terminology sometimes has double meanings. I want to share some of the experiences I had with computers, technology, and misunderstandings.

Technical Support:

During a technical support call, I told a customer over the phone to open a window, meaning a computer window. I overhead them put the phone done and actually open the window in their house. Or when installing software, sometimes you get the prompt, "Hit any key" and they would ask me, "Where is the any key???"

TIP: For those of you who don't know, the "any key" is any key on your computer keypad.

Demos:

I was working with my new boss in setting up the demo room and we had to plug in some computers. Usually demo rooms are dimly lit anyway but maybe in this circumstance the lights may have been dimmer than usual. However, in setting up the equipment, my boss would pass a cable to me to plug in and as he did so...He asked me, "Is it in???" I answered, "I think it is in but I can't feel it." After I said that, we realized how that sounded to the outside world of people walking by the demo room. (Nothing like really getting to know your new boss :>)

Another time my company sent me for a one-week training course to learn the Unix Operating System. My professor was rather dull, and to prove it, he mentioned to the class that he just doesn't feel right unless he does a hundred lines of code every night. When I got back to my corporate office for a meeting, I was speaking with our new Vice President of the company and mentioned my Unix class. I told him that the professor said, "I don't feel right unless I do a hundred lines of code every night." My Vice President had a very shocked look on his face and then said to me, "Your professor said he doesn't feel right unless he does a hundred lines of Coke every night???" I explained what I really said and we had a pretty good laugh.

TIP: Please enunciate clearly when speaking to the Vice President of your company as he might get the wrong idea.

My Name is Baaaaahbra

When I first moved to Northern California, I wanted to open a bank account and picked a bank at random. I went to the woman in new accounts and told her my name was Barbara Gross. She didn't spring into any kind of action and looked as if she was looking for hidden cameras or something. I was very confused by her actions as I was trying to give them money not the other way around. Finally, she asked to see my driver license and realized I was, in fact, Barbara Gross. She thought someone was playing a practical joke on her as the branch manager of the bank was also named Barbara Gross.

This other Barbara Gross later went on to become General Manager of a hotel downtown where I frequented a very popular restaurant on the ground floor. I later went to the restaurant and ended up speaking to the manager at the bar. He said that anytime I needed a reservation, I could call him. I said to him, "Why would I need to call you as my name is Barbara Gross."

I was single and she was married. When guys would be looking for me by calling information for my number, they sometimes got her husband who would answer the phone. Sometimes, I would get her medical results for tests. One time I received an invitation to an event for the Chamber of Commerce. I thought to myself that I would check it out and maybe meet her but we only crossed paths virtually.

Just for fun:

Interesting Conversation Starter:

If You Were An Inanimate Object, What Would You Be???

I don't know why I have thought about this but if I was an inanimate object, I would be a radio and the reason is this...

For whatever reason, sometimes a tune comes in my head. It was not the last song I heard or heard recently. For instance, an old song, "Mr. Sandman" came into my head while I was at work one day sitting in the same room as a co-worker. I started to hum the tune, and then I left the room for about five minutes. When I came back to the room, my co-worker was humming the "Mr. Sandman" song so I asked why she was singing such an old-fashioned song and she told me she had no idea. What would you be and why???

Attending Trade Shows:

Below are some pictures of men I have met while attending Trade Shows:

Pillsbury Doughboy: When I met him, he pinched me and I said he was "fresh".

Towel Dispenser Man: You never know when you might need to dry your hands.

Ketchup Man: I actually prefer mustard but he was not available.

My company usually made me the actress when we would have a stage presence at computer trade shows. One year we decided that we would hire a magician from Las Vegas and the show would be about how I could complete five tasks in my software before the magician could get out of his straight jacket and locks, and of course, I would always win. It was a lot of fun to do and we would put on this show every hour to bring people into our booth. At a break, I was speaking with the magician's wife and she said to me that every time she has to tie up her husband with the thick ropes, they cut her hands, I responded with a very serious face, "Yes, that happens to me when I tie my boyfriend up with ropes." It took her a few seconds to realize I was only kidding!!! My company also liked to give awards and I was given my own Oscar. Okay, it might not be exactly like the real one but it is priceless to me!!!

TIP: Keep showing up in your life as you never know when you will receive your next Oscar.

My Worst Day:

I once worked for a company who was taken over by another company and even though I knew that I was going to keep my job, I had to interview with the new owner. My new boss said to me that he was observing me and noticed that I was always happy. He said he wanted to know what my worst day was so I proceeded to tell him what next came into my mind...

The night before, I went to a party with cloth shoes and the shoes got dirty. I thought I would bring them to work with me the next day, so after work, I could go to the dry cleaners to get them cleaned, if possible. After work, in a lot of traffic, I finally made it to the dry cleaners and they proceeded to tell me they don't do shoes.

I then decided to treat myself to my favorite Chinese Food. Well, you know when you haven't eaten all day and you smell the food you love while stuck in traffic driving home; you can't wait to eat that food as soon as possible. I proceeded to park in my driveway and as I reached to pick up the bags of Chinese Food, it was too late to realize that the juices had leaked through the paper bags and the bottom of the bags opened on my business suit and silk blouse. I am now wearing the food I was dying to eat.

I then proceeded to my front door where I found a note which said that some construction workers drilled into my water main and I would not have any water until the next day. So, I am standing outside my front door, holding the note in my hand, wearing the food I desperately wanted to eat, holding my dirty shoes, had no water, and realized I had a choice, I could laugh or cry. I chose to laugh standing there all by myself.

I then changed my clothes and went to a dry cleaner around the corner from house to have my suit, blouse and shoes cleaned. It so happened that a very cute guy was standing right next to me as I am holding all of my dirty clothes and I knew he probably thought that I had thrown up on myself instead of it being Chinese Food. My new boss then said, "If that was your worst day, you are really the happiest person I know."

TIP: As Dale Carnegie says, "When life gives you lemons, make lemonade."

Home Purchase:

After renting for over twelve years, I decided to buy a townhouse. The first real estate agent I found, told me to look in the paper and check out the properties by myself and if I decided I liked something to call her. I thought to myself, if I am doing all that, what do I need a real estate agent for??? I decided to find a new one and I found a great one who is now a close friend of mine.

Initially, we looked at a number of properties that weren't exactly my cup of tea. We actually made an appointment with a woman to look at her house and were running a little late, so we called her to let her know. She said that she could probably wait ten more minutes but to come as soon as possible. We later found out that her water just broke and she was ready to give birth but was going to stay home as long as she could to show her house. She had a real incentive to sell but I did not have real incentive to help her give birth.

For my next opportunity, my real estate agent, Anna, told me to go to an open house on a Sunday. She had already checked out the property and believed that it was exactly what I was looking for. I had never been to an open house and didn't know quite when they opened for viewing. I wanted to make sure I was the first one there so I got there at around 9:00 am. I walked up to the front door and rang the bell and no one answered the door. I continued knocking and still nothing happened so I called Anna and got her voice mail. I asked her if she was sure of theaddress as no one was answering the door. Anyway, I didn't know what to do so instead of driving all the way home; I decided to go shopping at the supermarket around the corner. After shopping, I went back to try to view the open house again and still no answer. I called Anna again and left her another voice mail.

Well, I thought no sense just sitting in my car. I will drive home and wait for Anna to call me back. Anna finally called me back at noontime and said that open houses don't normally start until after noon on a Sunday. Additionally, the owners were probably still in bed sleeping. Luckily for me, they never saw my face or at least I didn't think they did.

I proceeded to go back to view the open house and when I got there, there was still no answer at the door. I called Anna again and got her voicemail. I then rode around the neighborhood to make sure that I was in the right place and made one last try to see if the property was available for viewing. I then caught a glimpse of a man running to the door with a sign in his hand. I was hoping he was the one who would open the door for me so I could take a view. I was in luck!!! He apologized for being late and opened the door and as soon as I walked in, I knew this was my dream house.

I called Anna immediately and we set up an appointment to meet the next day to put on offer on the property. As it turned out, even though the man was so late in showing the property, four other people were turning in offers, as well. It was now a bidding war. It was decided that we would all make our offers on the same day and the best offer would win. The day Anna was to make our offer, she had another client she was dealing with that caused us to be somewhat late. Luckily for me, Anna knew the seller's agent, Tom and we made it there in time to give our offer. Nervous wasn't the word for what I was feeling. Anna had to give her presentation of our offer while I waited in another room. While in this room all by myself, I was praying to my grandmother and other relatives now deceased to see if they could help me in any way in becoming the new homeowner. When Anna came in to tell me the news, she said, "We lost it." I was so sad to hear this news when she said, "I'm only kidding, we just have to wait for their answer." So **now** we waited for the final decision. About ten minutes later, Tom knocked on the door and said that my offer and one other offer are about the same and would like us to come up with a higher $$$ offer. The offer with the highest $$$ number will be the new owner.

Anna said to him that was not the original deal inferring that we may take our offer away (however, I was not going to do that). She told him that was plain greedy but he said that is what his seller wanted him to do. Well, I am not made out of money but we needed to come up with a better $$$ offer. While we were deciding this, there was a knock on the door and it was Tom again. I thought he was going to ask us what our new $$$ offer was but instead, he held his hand outstretched to me and said, "Congratulations, you are now the owner." My immediate response was, "Can I hug you???" and so I did. Then, I went to the sellers and hugged them, as well.

When all was said and done, our initial offers were fairly similar. The sellers opted for not getting overly greedy by asking us to come up with a higher dollar amount and decided to pick my offer!!!

TIP: Things happen for a reason.

Chapter 9
Las Vegas

I needed to go to Las Vegas for work on a business trip that needed to be scheduled at the last minute. The best hotel that we could find I will refer to as "El Roncho." I brought all my most expensive suits for the show that I was attending and have a habit when traveling of putting each suit in its own plastic bag and hanger so it won't wrinkle.

Since I was going to be in Las Vegas for the week, even though the hotel was a dump, I made plans with my friend, Nina, to stay until Sunday so we could go gambling at some nice places like Caesars Palace etc...

It was now Saturday night and the trade show was over. Nina and I dressed up and walked through the lobby wearing our finest garb. We were especially noticed as we walked through the El Roncho lobby as most of the guests were very casually dressed. We gambled until about four am at Caesars Palace and then went back to our hotel and fell in to bed as we had to check out the next day by noon.

As I opened my eyes in the morning, I noticed that in my closet all my suits were missing. The odd thing was that all of the plastic bags were still hanging neatly on their hangers, however, all the clothes were missing except my casual clothes. I initially thought Nina was playing a practical joke on me and I asked her what she had done with my clothes. She, being still half asleep, didn't know what I was talking about and seemed to be getting irritated at my questions until she looked at my closet and realized I was telling the truth. She then checked her clothes and all of her nice clothes were missing, as well.

We called security immediately and who showed up was a man about eighty-five years old. We told him the whole story and we had to keep repeating it as either he was too hard of hearing or kept forgetting what we were telling him. We checked and it did not look like anyone had jimmied the door so we determined it had to be an inside job. We believed that when the staff saw us leave the hotel, they knew they had all the time in the world to try on the clothes and take whatever they wanted.

After taking a long time with the security guard in telling him the story, he later told us that he could do nothing and we had to speak to the manager.

The manager said, "You have to prove gross negligence."

I said, "I understand if I left jewelry or money in the room, it would be my fault if anything was stolen. However, are you saying that once I check into a room and am ready to go out, I am supposed to check all of my clothes in a safe deposit box???"

He said, "Well, how do I know you even brought these suits in the first place???"

I said, "Well, if I knew I was supposed to take pictures of my outfits before I checked in to prove what I brought with me, I would have done so."

I really got upset but knew that this hotel was not going to do anything for me and I learned that it does not pay to stay in an establishment that is not going to do the best they can to resolve an issue such as this, so off we went to the airport.

While we were in the cab on the way to the airport, we retold our story to the cab driver. He told us just a week ago, two brothers had won the jackpot, had the money with them in their room and while they were asleep, someone came in and stole their money. He said that we had to report our incident to the Las Vegas Police in the airport, so we did. Sgt. Mayberry got very upset as he tried to find out from the hotel who was on duty the evening our clothes were stolen and got a runaround. He was very apologetic as he said this is very bad for tourism in Las Vegas.

Nina and I knew we were not going to come back for a small claims court date, however, as we were taking off up in the air, I turned to Nina and said, "I can now say, I literally lost the shirt off my back in Las Vegas!!!"

The good news is that my company ended up reimbursing me for me loss.

TIP: If you find a great company to work for, stick with them. And be careful of the hotels you select.

Buffets:

Anyone who knows me knows I love buffets. I have no shame at a buffet. One of the first things I will do if they have shrimp is load my plate and make a little mountain. A shrimp goes in and a tail comes out until all that is left on my plate is a big pile of shells. I actually think that some buffet owners think they will make a lot of money because I am petite. I typically surprise them by how much I can and do eat…especially at buffets. This one particular evening, after finishing my first plate, I decided that I wanted to go with a whole new selection. I turned around and saw that the table behind me had finished so I left my plate on their table so I could start with a new one. Once I returned to my table with my fresh plate, my friends couldn't stop laughing. It seems that the table behind me, that I thought had gone, really didn't leave the restaurant but just went for some new items all together. So, when they returned to their table and saw my plate, one at a time each one of them was asking the other if that was their plate. I really couldn't admit what I did to the other table and give myself away at that point after I created such confusion for the other party.

TIP: *Sometimes you just have to learn to keep quiet.*

Chapter 10
Having It My Way

Ordering Food in Restaurants:

I really try to be nice about it and don't ask for any ingredient that's not available on the menu (except in one instance). For example, if I was to order a salmon entre from the menu, I would order it in the following way: "I will have the garden salad with no croutons and dressing on the side. Can you blacken the salmon and give it to me plain with no sauce and just give me steamed vegetables, if possible???" Everyone at my table would tend to roll their eyes and say, "Oh Barbara." However, once they saw what my plate looked like compared to theirs, they would inevitably say my dish looked better than theirs and most likely copy me next time.

After the dinner, I usually say, "I hated it" with a straight face, however, if you looked at my plate, it looked as if I licked it as I liked it so much. It may take the waiter a few seconds to look down and then give me a big smile.

TIP: If you are paying for it, try to have it your way.

Standard Ordering Procedure:

Unlike most people, I like to eat the same thing for dinner every day until I get sick of it and then move on to something else that I will eat every day. When going to different ethnic restaurants, I order the same thing and never have to look at a menu. For instance, when ordering Thai food, I will always order Ginger Chicken. At one restaurant that I would frequent quite a bit, I was known as the Ginger Chicken Lady as when ordering food to go, I ordered eight orders of

Ginger Chicken so they asked me how many people??? I thought to myself, why are they asking me how many people, just give me eight orders of Ginger Chicken. (The reason they were asking how many people was that they wanted to know how much rice to give me.) I told them that they should know by now that I don't eat rice as I try to be a high protein gal and "yes" all of the food is for me. They assumed I was eating it all in one meal.

Lunch with Mom:

My mother and I are very close, just like best friends. I confide in her all of my stories including stories about my boyfriends, even the intimate parts, once I graduated college. My friends would say, "You tell your mother that???" and my mother would say, "You tell your friends that???" I just laugh as there really is nothing wrong with it. I'm pretty much an open book.

One day, while at lunch, I preceded to tell my mother about my latest relationship. As I started getting into the intimate content of the story, I realized from the corner of my eye that the couple next to us was about ready to fall on the floor as they were leaning so far over to listen to our conversation. I decided to beef up the content a little as my mother noticed the eavesdroppers, as well. We didn't let on that we knew they were listening as it was even more fun to make up outrageous things as I went along with the story.

TIP: If you feel like people are eavesdropping on your conversation, have fun with it.

New York Moment:

I was in New York City during a major blackout. I really lucked out as I was in walking distance of my hotel and right next door was a very fine restaurant. Since I was in New York on an extended stay because of business, I became a regular. The day of the blackout was very hot and muggy. People were looking for a place that was cool, had light and some beverages. As I walked up to the restaurant, I could see the manager pointing to people that he would allow in. It was just like trying to get in to Studio 54. Luckily, being a regular customer, really paid off and I was let in. My company was worried about me as the phones were dead and then my boss said, "I wonder who would be more in danger, Barbara because she is in New York City in a blackout or New York City because Barbara is there during the blackout."

I finally went back to my room around one am. There was still no power by the time I awoke in the morning so I had to start looking for food. The only place I could find was a pizza place that had a line around the corner but I knew I had to wait. When it came time for me to order, I ordered four pizzas and three salads as who knew when the power was going to come back on??? As soon as I got back to my room, there was power once again.

TIP: You can never have enoughpizza.

Ordering Food When Traveling:

I may initially get some funny looks from the staff as I order my food but once I explain why I am doing it, people understand and think about doing it themselves. Just call me the "Idea Woman".

There really isn't any good food available to eat while on an airplane these days, so as a former Brownie (I am always prepared). I have become famous for ordering food in one state or country and bringing it with me to another. On my last trip flying from San Jose to Chicago, I ordered: four hamburgers with lettuce, tomato onion, no bun, with mustard on the side. So, the food will stay in good condition in their skimpy package container, I ask that all of the vegetables be in one container and the burgers in another. Another reason I do this is because especially when you are flying west to east, by the time you get to your destination, all the restaurants are usually closed. I don't know about you but I cannot sleep on an empty stomach.

TIP: Always have a plan, especially when traveling.

Dinner with Mom:

I once went to dinner with my mother and we were absolutely starving. I ordered a piece of grilled fish with steamed vegetables as I try to keep my girlish figure. We waited what seemed to be a lifetime for the food to arrive. Finally, my meal showed up and I see this piece of fish before me swimming in grease. There was no possible way I could eat this greasy meal but I was so hungry that I didn't want to take the time to send it back.

A bright idea occurred to me. I took my cloth napkin and proceeded to press down on the fish sopping up all of the grease. Once I dried up the fish sufficiently, I picked up my fork and as I was ready to take the first bite, the waitress came to the table and said, "Thank goodness you didn't start eating your meal yet as I gave you the wrong entree." She proceeded to take the plate of food that was in front of me and replace it with a new plate with a piece of nicely grilled fish (exactly what I ordered) and then dashed off. We watched as she swiftly made it to a neighboring table and watched her give a man the fish that I had sopped up and made totally dry.

Can you imagine this man's dining experience??? He probably would not recommend eating at that establishment again. There really wasn't enough time for my mother or me to say a word to the waitress before she made the exchange. All we could do was laugh.

Chapter 11
Traveling Adventures in the US

Baja California:

I love cruises and decided to take a Mother and Daughter cruise to Puerto Vallarta, Mazatlán and Cabo San Lucas. Once you get on the ship, the first thing they want you to do is to make sure you know the station where your lifeboats are and they do a drill. Each of us had to go to our room, find our life jackets and go to our emergency station. My mother and I got to our station and the guy in charge said my life jacket was not on correctly. I guess I had it on inside out and backwards. So, a fellow passenger, who was a fireman, fixed it for me. It turned out that there was a whole team of firemen that were taking this cruise so we became immediate friends. We had some drinks in Mazatlán that were in a very long container. As you are finishing the drink, they have the following warning written on the bottom of the glass: Warning: Some People May Look More Attractive After Finishing This Drink!!!

TIP: Pay attention to warnings.

First Class Trip:

My friend from sixth grade, Jackie, told me about a cruise that she was going on that would be a good deal as we could get a group rate with some other people she knew. The plan was that I would fly in to Miami a day earlier, stay overnight at a hotel with Jackie, to meet the cruise ship the next day.

Since, I had saved quite a few airline points, I was going to travel First Class. It happened to be President's Day Holiday (heavy travel day) in February and I was departing from the San Francisco Airport. I usually get to the airport very early and check my bag. Once I got through security, I could hear announcements for weather delays and cancellations as not only was there fog in San Francisco but bad weather in general around the country. Then the announcement came that I was dreading. My flight that I was supposed to connect with to Chicago had been cancelled and now they had to re-route me.

My First-Class Trip became a stop in Los Angeles and then I had to wait several hours in the Los Angeles Airport for a "Red Eye" flight in the middle of the night and then get designated to the dreaded middle seat. What a First-Class Trip??? I had nothing better to do in the airport than to talk to all of my friends on the phone and draining my battery. To make matters worse, since my bag was already checked in earlier, it went on a different flight and I would just have to find my bag when I arrived in Miami.

As you can imagine, I was wearing winter clothes as it was fairly chilly in San Francisco. Once I exited the plane, a wave of humidity hit me. It felt like a hundred degrees with 100% humidity. I now had to go on a mission to find my bag so I went to the baggage claim area but there was no one there as it was five am in the morning. I tried to find someone to talk to and finally found a janitor and asked him where the baggage claim area was for delayed bags. He told me that I had to walk the whole length of the terminal. I felt like I had walked a mile and I was so hot wearing my winter clothes. I had to keep pushing on because if I did not get to the ship by noon, it would sail without me. I finally see a closed door that has a sign "Baggage". I am thinking it is probably locked but no, I turned the doorknob and low and behold there were piles and piles of bags all stacked up. There was no one to help me so I just started climbing around the bags and I could not believe it!!! I found my bag!!!

I hailed a taxi to take me to the hotel but when I tried to check in to find my friend, Jackie, they said there was no reservation for her or me??? I checked all of the papers I had with me but all reservations were made under a group name that I did not know. Maybe I had the wrong hotel??? My phone was dead so I had to charge it in the lobby. I then called and woke Jackie on her cell phone to ask her room number so I could get a key and at least have some time to get a few hours in as a nap before going to the ship. I was praying she would answer her phone. She did but I woke her up at six am. I had her speak to the desk clerk so he would give me the key to the room. Then, I proceeded to the elevator, opened the door to the room and slowly walked in quietly when I heard the "Click". You know the "Click" sound when the door locks behind you once you are in the room.

Now that I am inside the room and the door has closed behind me, I am just going to find my bed. As my eyes adjust to the dark room, I look at one bed and see it is occupied (that's okay) but I then look at the other bed and that bed is also occupied (that is not good)!!! I quickly realized that I have been given the key to the wrong room and try to get out of there as fast as I can as I had awakened some people and they were screaming at me to get out. I then had to go back downstairs and call Jackie again to tell me what room she was in and had the manager make sure he gave me the right key. I now attempt to get in the correct room this time and this time it worked. Jackie was trying to get some sleep and I attempted to, as well. When it was time to meet everyone in the group to go to the ship, as soon as I came into the lobby, they all shouted and pointed their fingers at me and exclaimed, "That's her…She's the one!!!". As it turned out, the other friends in the group were all policemen that I had walked in on. I could have been shot as they all had guns but I live to tell the tale.

Had a good time but what a First-Class Trip!!!

TIP: Before you plan a First-Class Trip, make sure it is not a big traveling day with bad weather.

Golf Ball:

On another cruise to the Caribbean, with my four high school friends, we were on the sun deck and I asked my friend, Susan, if I could use some of her suntan lotion since I didn't have my own. She said, "Of course." This particular day, I was mostly under an umbrella. Later that evening at dinner, my ankle started to swell up and then appeared a blister that became the size of a golf ball. I asked Susan what number of sunblock she gave me and she replied, "I don't use sunblock, I use baby oil." I was ready to kill her as obviously, even though I was mostly under an umbrella, my ankle must have been sticking out. It really made it easy to meet guys so they could say, "How did that happen???" It was so embarrassing but the blister stayed for the whole duration of the cruise, however, it was a great conversation starter.

TIP: When asking for suntan lotion, even from someone that has known you long enough not to just give you baby oil, make sure you ask if it has sunblock. Or better yet…get your own sunblock.

Alligator in New York:

I was once staying in a hotel in New York City for business. The nightclub, located on the lobby floor of the hotel was "the place to be" at the time and there was always a waiting line to get in. However, since I was a hotel guest, I did not need to wait in line and I was allowed one guest.

I decided on my last night that I would check this nightclub out to see what all the fuss was about and proceeded to walk directly to the head of the line when two guys stopped me and asked if I could get them in. I thought to myself, "Oh, why not", however what I said to them was, "Well, if I get you in, what's in it for me???" They told me that they would buy me a drink so I said, "okay." As I proceeded to the front of the line with my two new male companions, the bouncer said to me that I could only bring in one person. I replied to him, "What am I supposed to do as I have two friends with me???" The bouncer let us in and the guys bought me a drink.

Then one of the guys started taking out all of these different colored magic markers and proceeded to start drawing on a cocktail napkin. As it turns out, one of my two new friends was an artist and was drawing me a picture. I asked him, "Would you please draw my caricature???" He said, "I only do alligators." I said, "What do you mean you only do alligators???" He said, "That's my trademark, I only do alligators." So, he proceeded to draw on the white cocktail napkin a picture of an alligator holding a drink with the New York skyline in the background and at the top of the picture had my name in block letters. He even signed it.

When I returned home, I was so impressed with this picture, I had it matted and framed. You wouldn't even know it was drawn on a cocktail napkin. Who knows, one day he might be famous and I now have an original Goldberg.

TIP: If you ever get a chance to get an original Goldberg, go for it, as it is just lovely.

Riding On A Train:

When I received a new position at my company, we were to meet in Chicago. My new co-worker suggested I take the train from the airport and told me the train stop for my destination.

When I arrived in Chicago, I thought, no problem and got my luggage, found the train and off I went. Then, I started listening to the conductor for my stop. It seemed I could hear very clearly, "We are now coming to..." Fine, what I could not decipher was the actual name of the train stop as every time the train stop name was mentioned, it sounded very muffled.

I started to get a little worried as it seemed we were going from the Blue Line to the Red Line to the Green Line as I was looking at the maps. Finally, a fellow passenger took pity on me, and asked me what stop I was looking for and told me he would let me know when we arrived at my stop. What a relief!!! The same thing happened to me when I was in England. Could there be a train conductor conspiracy to drive travelers mad???

TIP: *Be thankful for the kindness of strangers.*

Riding In An Airplane:

I always get to the airport in plenty of time in order to check my bag and go through security. This particular day, there were a lot of delays and cancellations. Sure enough, they announced my flight has been cancelled. I was now in the middle of a long line trying to get reassigned to another flight. Since I had nothing better to do than observe my surroundings, I was watching the ticket agent speak to the first person in the line and this is how the conversation went:

First Try: Ticket Agent, "Well, you won't be getting to Orlando today; however, we can put you up in a hotel, free of charge, in either Denver or Phoenix today and get you to Orlando tomorrow."

Passenger: "I want to go to Orlando."

Second Try: Ticket Agent, "Well, you won't be getting to Orlando today; however, we can put you up in a hotel, free of charge, in either Denver or Phoenix today and get you to Orlando tomorrow."

Passenger: "I want to go to Orlando."

I started to look at my watch as this was taking a long time to even get the first passenger reassigned. Then, another ticket agent came to help and a passenger, who was not even in line, cut in front of everyone and started speaking to the new ticket agent. The person who was supposed to go next turned around to us in line and threw up her hands but what was anyone going to do about it. I was just laughing with the guy in line in front of me as what else can you do. When it was finally my turn to speak with a ticket agent, I said in the same deadpan voice of the first passenger as a joke, "I want to go to Orlando" and we both laughed. ☺

TIP: If you are a captive audience, try to make the best of your situation.

I was once on a very short flight about 45 minutes. Before we were about to depart, the flight attendant made an announcement is rather a stern voice. He said, "Since this is a very short flight, we will be offering you cranberry juice or water, that's it." So, just to amuse myself, when he got to me, I said, "I would like a cup of coffee." I could see that he started to get red and the veins in his neck looked like they were about ready to pop. Obviously, he was not having a good day even before he met me. He was about ready to yell at me thinking I did not listen to his announcement. However, he saw me crack a little smile and then he realized that I was only kidding with him. So, he then decided to ignore me and not only did he not give me coffee but he did not even give me water for the longest time. Finally, he did and when we were ready to land, I was trying to give him my cup and he kept ignoring me. Everyone, including the flight attendant had a good laugh!!!

TIP: You can make things fun, even in the most routine situations, about drink ordering.

Flight Attendant Initiation:

I was once on a very small plane and as we were about to land, a young flight attendant started to jump up and down in the aisle. All the passengers were questioning what she was doing??? She was told by the pilots that they were having trouble with the landing gear and needed her help. That was her initiation on her first flight.

TIP: Just in case you were wondering, pilots are the only people that can move the landing gear.

Renting A Car:

I needed to rent a car and I was in a very long line. I don't know about you, but I always feel better when I can turn around and find more people behind me that in front of me. Finally, it was my turn. So, while Mr. Rent-A-Car, Ben, was doing the paperwork, I asked him in a rather loud voice, "Ben, can I have the free upgrade???" Because I was not entitled to a free upgrade, Ben did not even look up from his paperwork. So, I proceeded to get my car, but before I entered the garage, I turned back to yell to Ben, "Thanks for the free upgrade." Now, of course, Ben did not give me the free upgrade but now everyone who was behind me in line thinks he did. One guy, found me in the parking garage before I left and asked me, "What did you say to Ben in order to get the free upgrade???" I replied, "I didn't!!!" What I have learned being in sales is why not ask for what you want, as the worst that can happen, is that you may get a 'no'. If it is something you want, it never hurts to ask.

Chapter 12
My Moscow Adventures

Do you choose to see the humor in the unexpected things as a challenge and an adventure??? How do you tend to see things??? I hope "My Moscow Adventures" will encourage you to embrace the adventure and humor in your own travels and life. No matter what comes, we can choose our response. Can I share with you some stories and experiences that had lots of opportunities to choose my response???

Five years ago, I was interviewing for a position as a Business Development Manager for a Computer Software Company. Initially, I interviewed at the local headquarters based in Northern California but ultimately, I was going to report to a woman at our International Headquarters based in Moscow. So, once the US Office decided I was a good candidate for this position, I had a couple of Skype calls with who would be my manager in Moscow and it was decided that I would be hired.

Once I was able to get all of my papers in order for a Visa, I was to fly to Moscow to meet everyone I would be working with in person. As the procedure goes, I needed to give my passport to a third-party company to generate and complete all of the paperwork for this Visa. My flights were arranged to travel to Moscow in March to give enough time for this paperwork to be completed. I was supposed to receive my passport, as well as, receive a new Visa before my flight.

When the package did not arrive at my office as scheduled, I called customer service to see if they could track the package. I gave them all the details and they told me that a supervisor would contact me within the hour. Needless to say, I never received a return phone call, even though they were informed that the package included my passport and that I had a flight the next day. I then started calling every hour to track the status of this package. It seemed that no one from this overnight mail service was taking any kind of ownership of this issue to even give me a courtesy phone call, to at least let me know, that someone was looking for this package. I would also like to emphasize that this particular document was MY PASSPORT WITH A RUSSIAN VISA.

In order for me to expedite getting a new passport, I ended up going directly to the San Francisco Passport Office. When you have had unexpected things happen and delays, how do you choose to respond??? Does your attitude become negative??? Do you get frustrated and stressed??? Or are you able to find humor in the situation and enjoy the journey and unexpected turns??? I think it's important to stop and check in on these things so that we are actively choosing who and how we want to be in the world no matter what happens to us.

My perseverance paid off and I did eventually make it to Moscow a month later. But this was just the beginning of my adventures in Moscow. (In looking back, perhaps these VISA challenges and delays were a timely reminder that things don't always go according to our plans.)

Two years ago, I was asked if after our corporate meeting, I would like to attend a party. Well, my middle name is 'party' and of course I signed up!!!

As I said, I signed up for a party but I didn't receive the agenda until weeks later. Since my airfare was already paid, there was no turning back. However, instead of just your average party, this event turned out to be an extreme sports adventure.

The agenda is as follows:

- ♦ Hiking up and down a mountainous river bed.
- ♦ Zip lining over a forest.
- ♦ Mountain climbing and rappelling.
- ♦ Diving into a river.

As I read about these activities, I started to get a little nervous as I am not the kind of person that would sign up for these kinds of activities. In fact, I don't even own a backpack. Even though everyone at my company can speak English, I can't speak Russian!!! So, if I got stuck in the middle of the zip line, I might still be there; but I had committed and when I commit to something, I do it. However, let me tell you, this agenda was completely out of my comfort zone.

Have you ever been faced with something like this??? Where you thought you signed up for something fun and familiar only to discover their definition of a 'party' is very different from your own. What do you do in those moments??? I discovered, I'll bring the party with me in how I show up, choose to laugh and embrace the adventure.

In addition, how we got to this campsite area was to take a two hour bus ride from Moscow to the airport, to take a two hour plane ride, to then take another two hour bus ride and then be loaded on a truck that looked like it came from World War II.

The only way I could get on the truck was to be pulled up by fellow colleagues as there were no steps and as they were pulling me up, they shouted to me to watch my head as I was getting in for fear I might just smack my forehead. Also, I guess I was not paying attention to all of the items I needed to bring in order to survive in this wilderness, for instance:

- ◆ A light to wear on my head as there were no lights at the campsite. This was especially important when finding the outhouse. Oh, yes, the outhouse. There was no shower or toilet, just a hole in a very small hut (I can't even begin to explain the smell)!!! I also neglected to bring my own toilet paper as the campsite didn't provide any so I was constantly begging if someone could "spare a square".

- ◆ I did not bring a bathing suit and it turned out to be 100 degrees with 100% humidity. So, the coolest thing I had to wear were the clothes on my back that I left with from the USA. Long black leggings and a baseball shirt. During the first event of hiking up and down a mountainous river bed, I was sweating so much, I looked like I had been in the water only I hadn't, until we came to a waterfall and I just bent over and dunked my head in the water. Everyone was so proud of me that I had finally experienced the waters of Russia. For anyone that knows me, I either wear flip flops or heels as I love freedom of feet. My brother does not believe I even own a pair of sneakers just to give you an indication of how athletic I am. However, sneakers were mandatory for this adventure. During the course of the hike, the rubber from the bottom of my sneakers started to separate and flip off so I had to have a guy cut off the rubber bottoms with his pocket knife.

- ♦ They recommended bringing a backpack. Somehow, I missed that and brought my beautiful clutch purse to carry my things in throughout the adventure. I kept trying to keep the clutch tucked under my arm (as it didn't have handles) and eventually someone offered to carry it in their backpack.

Needless to say, after the first event, I decided to be the onsite photographer and let the others enjoy their sporting experience, while I participate in a 'bonding only experience' with the whole team. I found a way to participate and connect that was a little bit more in line with playing to my strengths in connecting, bonding, building community and relationships and let them have their athletic adventures.

I got to take this whole bonding thing to a whole new level as I shared a tent with two other co-workers. We were given sleeping bags to lie on the ground in our tent and I was in the middle. You just could not help to get to know one another better. I never took my one and only outfit off for the whole weekend as it was the coolest thing I could wear. The extra clothing, I packed was long sleeved as there was a possibility it could get very cold at night (it never did). However, even through my pants, the mosquitos were after me. When I say that every square inch of my body was bitten, I am not exaggerating. The only part of my body that was spared was my face. I believe the reason for that was that once the mosquito got close to my head, I could wave it off as I could hear them coming from the buzz in my ear.

The evenings were a lot of fun as we sat around the campfire singing songs for hours but I would just like to say again, I just signed up for a party!

If you learn anything from what I have just shared with you, go ahead, sign up for a party but make sure you see the agenda first and go with the flow. Decide to have a great time no matter what!!! In fact, be the party and bring the party with you!!!

The following year, my company was having another annual business meeting in Moscow for a team building event. This year I was going to be prepared!!!

I purchased clothes that had bug spray, extra bug spray, hats and even a net to put over my head!!! For fun, I actually wore the same outfit from the previous trip (the black leggings and baseball shirt) to joke around with them. I wanted to get a laugh when I stepped off the plane wearing the same outfit I had worn the entire party trip' letting them know I was ready.

However, things didn't quite go according to my plans. It turned out the joke may have actually been on me and not the other way around.

I always try to get to the airport in plenty of time to check my bag and go through security. This trip, I arrived at the San Francisco Airport in plenty of time, however, there was a very long line to check my bag. In addition, because this was an International Flight, I was told by my company that I could check my bag at a Domestic Airline in San Francisco and they would then transfer my bag to the International Airline directly to Moscow.

I rushed to the gate in San Francisco to find out that my flight was delayed for a half hour and to make matters worse, once I landed, I had to sit on the tarmac for another half hour. It turned out that the Los Angeles to Moscow Flight was delayed due to baggage problems. So, my colleague held a place for me in line and I was able to board the flight in time.

But, sadly, even though the Domestic Airline took my bag to check it through to Moscow…they did not deliver on their promise. What do you do when you count on someone or an organization and they don't come through as promised??? How do you choose to respond??? I found out later that it had been sitting at the San Francisco Airport for two days before they discovered that they needed to put it on the next International Flight to Moscow.

I would receive emails from the International Airline that the bag had arrived in Moscow, but when I called to see when they could deliver it to my hotel, they could not manage to find it??? I was wearing the same clothes for the whole time I was in Moscow about ten days. This started to feel very familiar, despite my careful planning.

I had four days of business meetings and four days of jeeping, horseback riding, motorcycling and team bonding exercises in the forest (sometimes in mud and sometimes in the pouring rain) so my boss generously shared her own sneakers, socks, sweater and raincoat. All in all, as each day passed, I just thought it was funnier and funnier!!!

My bag finally arrived the day before I was about to leave for the USA, just in time to make the return trip home with me. All of the special clothing I purchased for the trip (even though very wrinkled) still had all of the sales tags on as I was never able to wear them so the retail store let me return everything without question. They even let me return all of the bug spray and suntan lotion even though the boxes were totally smashed!!!

TIP: Read the agenda.

Chapter 13
Birthday Moments

Birthdays are very special to me as I believe everyone should be acknowledged at least one day a year. Once I meet someone and find out their birthday, I will send them a card every year. I have received comments from friends such as, "I haven't seen you in thirty years. You remembered my birthday and my wife forgot."

Here are some birthday moments I hold dear:

Old Spice:

My father would only wear cologne called "Old Spice". He would not wear anything else. Since the whole family knew he loved "Old Spice", he would receive it for his birthday time and time again. He had acquired a closet full of it. So, when his birthday would come around, instead of going to the store and buying him more "Old Spice", I would go into his closet and re-gift it to him. He never knew!!!

Danny:

My brother, Danny, sent me a birthday card that said, "You know how when we were growing up I made your life a living hell, well I'm not done yet." Years later, he forgot he sent me that card and sent the same one again. I believe Danny was very influential in building my sense of humor.

Family Birthdays:

My family has always made it a point to get together for birthdays and since most of our birthdays are in the springtime, we celebrate everyone's birthdays at the same time. We used to go out and get gifts and everyone would say they loved what they got and then return the stuff for something they really liked and it was a known joke in our family. So finally, we decided that we would not do gifts anymore as we really just wanted to get together as a family and celebrate and have a good meal.

We would always have our birthday celebrations in San Diego as that is where my mother lives. I would fly down earlier to spend a little extra time with my mother. One year, my mother said that she would like to go shopping as she needed a few items. While we were shopping, she said, "I like this blouse." I looked at the blouse and said, "I like this blouse."

Then, a funny idea came to me. I would buy the same blouse for me, my mother and sister-in-law. Now, I know we had a rule about "no gifts" but this was too funny.

However, I now had to find a gift for my brother. Since he is a diver, I would always get him diver toys that could swim and I looked all over for one but good not find anything.

Then, I found a holder for a woman's necklace in the shape of a penguin. I did not buy this item for the necklace but the penguin was the closest thing I could find to diving???

Traumatized:

My mother once asked me if I was ever traumatized growing up. I knew she was looking for something to feel guilty about. As far as I was concerned, I was given a charmed life growing up and I am forever grateful. But I needed to give her something so this is what I said, "Well, after all, my name is Barbara and you bought me plenty of dolls. Chatty Cathy, Tressy, Serenade, Barbette, Barbie's cousin and Midge, Barbie's friend, but you never bought me a "Barbie". She was sure she did but I said she did not. The following year, without using any words, my mother presented me with a wrapped oblong box. I knew what it was immediately without even opening it and started to cry (good cry). I told all of my friends the story and the next year, my friend, Aileen, presented me with a wrapped oblong box for my birthday, I opened it up and it was "Ken". I started to cry again and it was (good cry).

My friend, Sue, was also very creative when buying me birthday gifts. I had a big party and I would open each gift and pass it around for everyone to see. When I opened Sue's gift, I saw kitchen magnets. As most of my friends know, every time I go somewhere or my mother goes somewhere, we buy each other the same kitchen magnet but they have to be outstanding. So, as I was looking at the kitchen magnets that Sue gave me as a gift, they really were not that special. I saw an alarm clock and a baby crying and as I passed her gift for everyone to look at it, I exclaimed to Sue, "I love it!!!" She said, "No, you don't. You did not look at the whole thing." They passed the gift back to me and then I saw the joke. The theme was, "Things That Are Loud". An alarm clock, a baby crying and then I saw kitchen magnets of me. Here are some pictures:

TIP: Be aware of the details and enjoy the fun.

Chapter 14
My "Granny"

I would like to honor my grandmother, Annie Rosen, as because of her light, I was shown the true meaning of unconditional love and to be able to laugh and enjoy life to its fullest!!!

Annie was born in 1892 in Russia and came to the USA in the early 1900s. She met and married Myer who also arrived in the USA about the same time. Myer and Annie had two daughters, first Lil and six years later, Esta. Lil married Eddie and had two boys and a girl. Esta married Benny and had two boys and a girl. My grandmother showed us the beauty and importance of always making sure that our families would stick together.

We always shared every holiday and birthday celebration together at my Aunt Lil and Eddie's house as they had a basement for parties. My father was a pioneer, as he bought a video camera that captured all our celebrations, minus the sound. Every chance our family got while together, we would watch our old home movies which were only of interest to us, but never bored us, as we could watch these movies time and time again to relive the moments.

But now let me tell you more about my personal relationship with the loving Grandmother, Annie. I don't know how many of you know the show, "The Beverly Hillbillies," but once I heard that family call their Grandmother, ""'Granny'"", I started calling my Grandmother, ""'Granny, as well.

I am just not the youngest of my immediate family but the youngest of our whole extended family. Since I was so much younger than my siblings and cousins, by the time I came on the stage, I was known as "the baby". To this day, no matter how old I get, I am still "the baby". So, my grandmother became my best friend and played all sorts of games with me from picking the fastest raindrop, board games or card games. It seemed that every time I played cards with "Granny", I would win!!! (I felt like a success!!!) I had no idea she was letting me win each time. One time, "Granny" won by accident and she started to laugh uncontrollably. I really did not think this was funny and it hurt me deeply that my "Granny" would laugh at me. That was the day I found out I was not invincible and I was crushed, but in hindsight, it is hilarious!!!

We would go everywhere together as I just loved being with her. She always made me feel so special and let me know that I could do anything I set my mind to accomplishing so I always hoped she would be proud of me. I also watched how loving she was with everyone in our family. She was always right there to be supportive, for her family.

What I learned from her was to always be supportive, in any way I could, to help someone in need. I have been so blessed to know unconditional love and having the feeling around me of such security that I want to extend a hand to someone who did not have the benefit of my upbringing.

Once I was in junior high school, my mother started working during the day so when I came home from school, I would sit and watch the soap operas with "Granny" and get involved with all of the characters. She had a hearing aid and for no apparent reason at random moments, it would give off this high-pitched piercing sound. She could not hear it and I would have to shake her to tell her to fix it!!! Here, I learned how to laugh at the unexpected as many things will happen in life and it is how you choose to react to every situation.

When she stayed overnight, she would put her teeth in a glass in the bathroom. I would also tease her if she ever lifted her arm wearing a sleeveless dress, as I would shake the loose skin below and she always laughed. I think if someone were to do that to me, I would get pretty irritated but not her. She taught me about intention as she knew I loved her and that was my way of being playful.

She could always make me laugh. One day shopping, she found a dress in a bag. Yes, that is how you bought it and a "big selling point". The dress was made of nylon material that you could roll up in a bag and when you opened the bag, the dress was perfect, not one wrinkle. She loved it!!! Here, I learned that it doesn't matter what everyone else is wearing or doing but what suits you. It is really very fun and satisfying the more you can embrace your authentic self.

She knew me very well so she knew I was a very picky eater. When my Aunt Lil would have parties, she would have very nice food on the buffet table but I really liked little hotdogs and meatballs. I could not get enough of them and actually it was a lot cheaper that the other items on Lil's table. Well, one-time Lil forgot to make my favorites and I started picking at her buffet table and putting things back on the buffet table after I decided I didn't like it. When, new guests came to the buffet table and saw some of the piles of food I put back on her very organized and fancy table, they were to say the least, not very interested in tasting the food. Once, they figured out the culprit, I was taken away from the table. Instead of getting angry at me, "Granny" said, "Lil, you should have made Barbara the hotdogs and meatballs."

From then on, hotdogs and meatballs were always on the menu for me.

Speaking of meatballs, when I got my first puppy, he got sick and "Granny" thought that it would be a good idea to bind his stomach if he ate boiled meatballs. Of course, it was not the meat of the highest quality but they were meatballs and she made them for my sick puppy and cured him. This filled me with joy as even though my "Granny" did not care for my puppy as much as I did, she would go out of her way to find a solution. She was always looking for the benefit of others and being so selfless. I was always in such awe of her and aspire to her virtues.

Once, I took a sewing class and let me just say, I knew early on that sewing was not going to be something I excelled at, however, I did make a nightgown for "Granny", that hung a little crooked. She loved the fact that I made her a nightgown and to her it was perfect!!! **She wore it every night she slept over at our house and it would just make me laugh.**

I will just face the facts that I am not artistic when it comes to knitting, ceramics, painting (well, maybe I am okay with paint by numbers) but that did not matter to "Granny" as she thought everything I did was fantastic!!! If you have a choice to make someone feel better or worse about something with no real consequence, why not choose to make them feel better.

I was and can be a pretty good baker/cook when I want to be. She passed down some recipes that we still love to eat to this day. One of my favorites was potato pancakes. I would let you know the recipe but it is still a secret.

She attended every dance recital I had, as well as, was the first person to be in the car when I got my driver's license. She was not afraid. It would always fill my heart about how much I knew that she loved me and how much I loved her.

"Granny" died when I was about fourteen years old. I was just devastated. There are really no words to express my loss for the woman who was always on my side, no matter what!!! But at least she died peacefully in her sleep. I believe in quality of life and also making sure there are no words left unsaid. It was always love.

I once went to a psychic as a birthday present from some of my friends. I asked the psychic, "Since I was so close with my "Granny", I was wondering when I hear a noise in my ears, does that mean that she is thinking of me???" The psychic closed her eyes for a moment as if to converse with my "Granny" and then replied, **"How could you even ask that question. Don't you know that for her the sun rose and set on you???"** I just started to cry with joy.

Each year that I get older, I have found myself to be more spiritual. My belief today is that we come into this life to learn a new virtue and to experience this life's sole purpose. I believe in this life that my soul purpose is to be able to show other people the gift of laughing at everyday living and be your true authentic self as my "Granny" had shown me.

After all of these years have passed, to me, she has never left my side. I believe that she is watching me or is guiding me in my travels through life or could very well be connecting with me in this life in some other form.

I try to say the following affirmation as often as I can. I think this affirmation comes from the values extended to me from my family and especially from my "Granny":

1. I am unconditionally loved
2. I am healthy
3. I am wealthy
4. I am successful
5. I am happy
6. I am my true authentic self
7. I am grateful

…and then I pinch myself as that just makes me laugh!!!

TIP: Remember to do something that will make you laugh!!! Carry the legacy of light, laughter and joy forward!!!

Reviews

Elizabeth Bachman

Humorous Adventures with Baaaaabra is a delight from beginning to end. Full of stories, full of tips, full of laughter. Barbara Gross gives us insights into how to turn the accidents of life into humor.

If you want to fill your life with light, laughter and joy, this is the book for you!

--Elizabeth Bachman, The Star Maker for Speakers

(415) 967-1014

ElizabethBachman.com
https://www.facebook.com/ElizabethBachmanStarMakerForSpeakers

https://www.linkedin.com/in/elizabethbachman/?trk=hp-identity-name

https://twitter.com/Starmaker4spkrs

https://www.youtube.com/watch?v=dPc2Mvlu-UM

Orly Amor

"One anecdote after another, made me feel like I was reading a memoir full of little adventures. Barbara takes you on a roller coaster of emotions that give light to everyday situations in the big school of Life. A fun and easy read. Well worth it."

-Orly Amor, International Public Speaker, Bestselling Author Founder of the HWNCC.com

917.515.6803

orly@orlyamor.com

www.orlyamor.com

https://www.facebook.com/OrlyAmorcom/

https://twitter.com/Iamorlyamor

Bonnie Bruderer

This book is fantastic for anyone that wants to improve communication skills. Barbara shares deeply personal, authentic examples of situations that occurred and does a great job of extracting the learnings, so that others can benefit.

Bonnie Bruderer, Founder, bingenetworks.tv

CEO/Founder BINGE Networks

www.bingenetworks.tv

800.476.5837

Rosie Bank

Barbara Gross makes light out of life by bringing humor to everyday situations. Her outlook is delightful and her stories in this book made me smile. I enjoyed the author's life experiences and how she uses them to help us on our own journey. Finding what is funny is a great recipe for making life easier and more fun. Thanks to Baaaaahbra for reminding me to do this in my life.

-Rosie Bank, Founder Health Matters Coaching

www.GetYourBodyToLoveYouBack.com

www.RosieBank.com

650-740-9500

Rosie@RosieBank.com

Joanne Weiland

Want to feel happier and lighter? Watch, read or listen to Baaaaahbra. You will find her on stage, TV, Radio or grocery store. She's everywhere!

Baaaaahbra's exuberant personality is filled with laughter, love and joy. Baaaaahbra's unusual everyday situations are hysterical! Baaaaahbra's adorable accent makes me smile.

You'll love her book: **"Humorous Adventures with Baaaaahbra" – sidesplitting!**

Together you will

-walk through her amazing life

-grasp why things happen

-understand what happens in Vegas does NOT stay in Vegas

-experience traveling with Baaaaahbra, even to Moscow!

-find the key to why we are here…..

Baaaaahbra radiates light from the inside out.

Joanne Weiland, Chief Collaborations Officer
jweiland@LinktoEXPERT.com
www.JoanneWeiland.LinktoEXPERT.com
www.LinktoEXPERT.com

John Hall

When I first met Barbara (soon to be known to me and the rest of the world as Baaaaahbra), I knew that I was in the presence of someone very special. Her sense of humor about life is indeed infectious- and she captures that unique view of life for all of us throughout the pages of her book. From her anecdotes about misunderstandings due to her captivating Boston accent to her life experiences through the lens of humor, one can't help becoming immersed in the humorous approach to life events.

Her many personal tips throughout the text not only provide us with her special view of life (often with a chuckle), but actually provide thought provoking insights of life lessons that we can use in lightening up our own circumstances when life throws us a curve.

Life…with a refreshing side of humor…that's Baaaaahbra! ***"Humorous Adventures with Baaaaahbra!!!"*** is a joyful journey that is definitely not to be missed!

John Hall, MBA, LCDR USN (Ret)

Best Selling Author

Sailor180@hotmail.com

Deb Dutcher
--5 Stars—

Barbara Gross has a way of taking a mundane, everyday event and putting her "funny-bone" spin on it. She takes you through her life, with all the funny twists and turns. I especially like her stories about boyfriends, college, dates, job interviews and travel adventures.

They bring back long-forgotten memories of my own life. Take a walk with Barbara through *her* life, it is definitely an enjoyable trip!

Deb Dutcher, Author and Health Coach

www.sexyleanandstrong.com

650-400-2612 Mobile/Text

YouTube: https://bit.ly/1ScwzZm

FaceBook: https://www.facebook.com/deb.dutcher

Twitter: https://twitter.com/debdutcher

Instagram: @sexyleanstrongtv

Trisha Garrett

"Humorous Adventures with Baaaaahbra" is a delightful read. This book will make you laugh and keep a smile on your face long after you finish reading it as Barbara shares her journey.

Absolutely loved how she so skillfully weaved in the importance of communication. This book will bring joy to your heart and is a must read.

-Trisha Garrett

LifeYouDeserve.com

trisha@lifeyoudeserve.com

http://www.LifeYouDeserveAcademy.com

https://www.facebook.com/trisha.garrett77

Irma Vargas

Have you ever felt like you were living the story that the author was describing? This is what it was like for me when reading **"Humorous Adventures with Baaaaahbra"**. Reading this book was such a joyful ride with its descriptive scenes. Not only did the stories make me laugh but the stories of Barbara's life made me happy. They reminded me of the fun times I had with my own siblings and parents.

It isn't often that you read a book which provides such inspiration while making you laugh out loud. It is the story of a woman who has held on to the wonderful lessons of taking the bitter with the sweet and accepting that not everything is going to be hunky dory. There are going to be times that life throws us a curve ball and when it does refer back to the lesson taught in this book! Humor will get you through much of it and help you see the brighter side of life. Congratulations Barbara; you hit just the right note of fun and substance!

Irma Vargas, MPA, Certified StrengthsFinder Coach V1H Consulting

www.v1hconsulting.com

Info@v1hconsulting.com

Cynthia Stott

If you are looking for a book filled with humor and inspiration, then ***"Humorous Adventures with Baaaahbra"*** is for you. From sharing about how her accent and region choices of words has gotten her into trouble, to dating mishaps and how her grandmother taught her about unconditional love, Barbara keeps you in stitches and touches your heart. I love how all of her stories end with a tip or life lesson that is truly universal. I literally couldn't put this book down and my sides hurt from laughter. Great book for yourself or as a gift for someone special.

Cynthia Stott

International Speaker Coach/Global Visibility Mentor

www.CynthiaStott.com

Programs@CynthiaStott.com

415.298.7306

About the Author

I am from Massachusetts & after graduating college became a native Californian, however, my accent will have to be surgically removed.

My degree is in Education & I have been a teacher but I am currently a Business Development Manager for a computer software company & have been in the software industry since 1990.

I would like to express my love for life by showing people how being able to laugh at oneself is great fun!!!

When I tell my stories, I have been asked, "Why do all of these funny things happen to you???" & I reply, "If you listen carefully, they were not so funny at the time but in hindsight they were hysterical!!!"

I have learned that being my authentic self is what I want to be, & show others why that is valuable, as I have proven this to myself & others with the success I have achieved in life.

Contact Information:

baaaaahbra@baaaaahbra.com

(650) 575-4636

www.baaaaahbra.com

https://www.youtube.com/channel/UCTe05eh2e8D8-PLCOz-EFyw

https://www.facebook.com/baaaaahbra/

https://www.linkedin.com/in/barbaralgross

@baaaaahbra

Instagram: baaaaahbra_show

Bachelor of Science in Education from the University of Massachusetts in Amherst

President's Club Awards for Sales & Technical Expertise from Xerox Imaging Systems / ScanSoft

Vice President of Membership at ABBYY Talk ToastMasters Club in Milpitas, CA (4 years)

www.ingramcontent.com/pod-product-compliance
Lightning Source LLC
Chambersburg PA
CBHW072053290426
44110CB00014B/1662